THE FUTURE OF INDUSTRIAL MAN

THE FUTURE OF INDUSTRIAL MAN

A conservative approach

by

PETER F. DRUCKER

GREENWOOD PRESS, PUBLISHERS
WESTPORT, CONNECTICUT

HD
82
D7
1978

Library of Congress Cataloging in Publication Data

Drucker, Peter Ferdinand, 1909–
    The future of industrial man.

    Reprint of the ed. published by John Day Co.,
New York.
    1. Economic policy. 2. Industry and state.
3. Conservation. 4. Economic history—20th century.
I. Title.
HD82.D7 1978   338.9   77-28895
ISBN 0-313-20227-3

Reprinted with the permission of Thomas Y. Crowell Company

Reprinted in 1978 by Greenwood Press, Inc.
51 Riverside Avenue, Westport, CT. 06880

Printed in the United States of America

10 9 8 7 6 5 4 3 2

This book owes to my wife whatever clarity
of thought and unity of form it has. It is dedi-
cated to her in the hope that the work and care
which she lavished on it will not appear to her
to have been entirely in vain.

CONTENTS

CHAPTER ONE

THE WAR FOR THE INDUSTRIAL SOCIETY

THIS war is being fought for the structure of industrial society—its basic principles, its purposes, and its institutions. It has one issue, only one: the social and political order of the entirely new physical reality which Western man has created as his habitat since James Watt invented the steam engine almost two hundred years ago.

Nothing shows this more clearly than the fact that this is the first war really to be fought as an industrial war —as a war in which industry is not an auxiliary but the main fighting force itself. Any peace following this war must be an industrial peace—a peace in which industry is not just on the periphery of the peacetime social organization but is its center. For it is a law of political life that the peacetime and the wartime organizations of society must be based on the same principles and follow the same structural rules. At one time it may be war that creates, or at least crystallizes, the new society; at another, peace. The question which comes first is one of the oldest—and one of the most idle—speculations of political philosophy; and the practical politician may well feel that it belongs in the category of the "hen or egg" speculations. But as to the fact itself there is no doubt: war society and peace society must be of one piece. The industrial war society of today must lead to an industrial peace society of tomorrow.

During the last war it was still possible to look upon the industrial system and its social organization as mere subsidiaries. Not only were machine guns, airplanes, tanks and automobiles handled and mishandled as auxiliaries in the traditional pattern of infantry warfare. In its basic social unit the warfare of 1914 still mirrored a feudal organization of society; for the infantry company in which there is no division of function and of skills really traces back, almost unchanged, to the times when the squire rode out to war accompanied by his tenants and villeins on foot.

It is true that in its final stages the last war too had become an industrial war. The great material battles of 1917 and 1918 were industrial battles. Yet the last peace was not an industrial peace. And the social organization of the Western world between the wars did not solve the problem of the industrial society; it did not even attempt the solution. To this discrepancy may properly be attributed the collapse of the Versailles world. Versailles and the years after—up to 1929 and in most countries up to 1939—determinedly, though often un-

consciously, postponed and evaded a solution of the political and social questions of the industrial system.
There was a tremendous and forceful attempt to restore
what was basically a preindustrial society: that of 1913.
Fundamentally the people of this between-war world—
so near in time yet so completely incomprehensible in
spirit even to us who were of it—were only too well
aware of the discrepancy. This was shown in the insistence upon permanent peace as the one way to maintain
the social structure of the Versailles world.

To say that free society could not survive another
war—something few would have doubted in 1928 or
1934—was simply to say that free society as we knew it
was incapable of finding a social and political organization for the industrial system. Insofar as it meant anything, it was a sentence of death for free society, with
a major miracle the only reprieve. For permanent peace
belongs to the millennium rather than to any man-made
society. As it was, the death sentence came near enough
to being executed. It is not due to any reversal of the
appeasement feeling in the free countries, a feeling that
had its roots in the conviction that industrial war was inevitably the end of a free society, but to Hitler's basic
mistakes, that we can fight today for freedom.

At the next peace conference we may try again to establish permanent peace—though I think we have all
come to doubt the wisdom of such an attempt. But we

certainly cannot and will not shirk the solution of the basic political and social issues of the industrial system. The reality of this war—not to mention the reality of the postwar period—will make it impossible.

Today the industrial machines of war are autonomous and the center around which everything else is built. The infantry man has largely become a subsidiary source of power. The social power-relationship between a pilot and the crew of a bomber plane, or between the commander of a tank and his men is the same as that between a foreman and the gang on the assembly line. It is based as much upon a hierarchy of skills and functions as upon a hierarchy of command. The social difficulties in every army today, the inability to maintain the old forms of discipline, the old system of promotion and the old ranking according to seniority instead of industrial skill, are expressions of the fact that the old preindustrial society of the army is inadequate to organize and to master the new industrial social reality. In every army today the old social forms give way to new ones— a change which has been most drastic in the Nazi Army and to which that army owes much of its fighting strength and morale. And in the society of tomorrow the old social forms of a preindustrial age will have to give way to new forms of an industrial society.

Every historian knows that the necessity to organize their armies on the new social pattern of the French armies forced Prussia and Austria during the Napoleonic Wars to accept the basic social principles of the French Revolution. The historian of tomorrow will see that it was the need to organize our war effort on the basis of the industrial system which will have forced our generation to develop an industrial society. It is the privilege and the responsibility of our generation to decide on what principles this society is to be based.

This has nothing to do with the question whether participation in a war is good or evil. Nor do I assert that war is meaningful, creates anything, or solves anything. On the contrary, I am convinced that in itself war is meaningless, creates nothing, and solves nothing. All I say is that war is a fact—one of the most important and undeniable facts, but still nothing but a fact. And facts in themselves are meaningless, create nothing, and solve nothing. They just exist. Whether they acquire meaning and, if so, what; whether they create or destroy; whether they solve anything and how—that depends on what we do with them.

It is certainly true that the first thing to do in a war is to win it. It is equally true, however, that we want to win in order to give our meaning to the war and the ensuing peace. With the questions: what is the issue, what is its meaning, and how can we find our solution, this book is exclusively concerned. It has but one topic: How can an industrial society be built as a free society?

Obviously I shall have little or nothing to say on post-war blueprints, on boundaries, international federations, the League of Nations or the gold standard. Not that I consider those practical problems of national and international organization to be of secondary importance. Such one-sidedness would be just as stupid as that of some of our blueprinters who think that the job is exclusively one of social mechanics. The one without the other—social mechanics without political principles and vice versa—is worse than useless; it is harmful. Sometimes concrete practical results grow immediately out of a discussion of ideas and principles. Sometimes an opportunistic, emergency invention, developed by a political plumber on the spot and without any thought of a general rule, gives birth to a new philosophy. In politics one must either be a dualist or nothing; hence the "realist" and the "idealist" exclude themselves from political effectiveness. However, this study will not try to develop concrete solutions for concrete situations, if only because this author has no idea what the concrete situations of the future will be. The only proper way to deal with concrete postwar issues today seems to me to draw up a multitude of alternative solutions for every possible job and every possible contingency—in the manner in which a general staff draws up a multitude of war plans in order to have one that will fit. This is a task which exceeds not only what can possibly be cramped into one book, but also what one man could possibly do in one lifetime. Furthermore, I see no way of discussing postwar issues as separate from those of the wartime itself. That day in the future at which we shall be able to make our peace appears to me to be a point where we change horses rather than the point at which we begin or end our journey.

In short, my task is to think through basic problems, to understand basic issues, to prepare new approaches from our existing basis of a free society. I do not pretend to know what the industrial society of the future will look like. I hope to be able to show how we can get there.

2.

Perhaps the most important—and apparently the most difficult—step in the preparation of a free and functioning industrial society is the realization that our crisis is one affecting the social and political foundations of the Western world. Totalitarianism grew out of a collapse of values, beliefs, and institutions common to all Western countries. And the present war is a civil war for the future of Western society which cannot—except in a purely military sense—be won merely by beating off the aggressors from without. This means that the solutions lie within our own society: in the development of new institutions from the old and tried

principles of freedom, in the emergence of new forms
for the social organization of power, and altogether in
the rethinking and re-forming of the basis of our society.
To understand the character and nature of the great up-
heaval of which this war is but the last and, I hope, the
final explosion, also implies the complete repudiation
of all those glib and superficial theories which see the
explanation for this war and for the threat of Nazi totalitarianism to our society, in the German (Japanese,
Italian) "national character," in the trend of German
history, or in specifically German beliefs or institutions.

It is not to be denied that these factors exist or that
they played an important part. The Versailles peace, the
German inflation, Hitler's frustrated boyhood in imperial Vienna—all these matter. But they only explain
how certain things are being done and by whom—not
why they are being done and to what end.

Undoubtedly Germany has been Europe's "geological
fault" for these last fifty years—the spot where every
disturbance results in an earthquake. But France played
the same part for a hundred years before. In either
case, there were profound reasons for the lack of balance, the propensity to tyranny, the lust for aggression.
They had nothing to do with national character. Totalitarianism could have happened in any industrial country; had it not happened in Germany first it would have

started somewhere else in Europe. That it came to power in the Germany of the Weimar Republic was undoubtedly due to certain factors unique to the Germany of the twenties. And a good many details of Hitlerism are peculiarly nineteenth or twentieth century German. But however striking and spectacular, both the uniquely German causes and the peculiarly German manifestations concern only externals. They explain the "how" and even the "when" of Hitlerism but give no answer to the question why it came and what it is.

French totalitarianism would undoubtedly be different from the German in its slogans, its concrete institutions, and its specific manifestations. And both would be very different from a Spanish or a Czech totalitarianism. But there would be little difference in the essentials if the basic principles which they accepted were the same. These principles are neither "inevitable" nor to be found in national character, history or institutional structure. They are chosen deliberately, and intentionally, and they are the choice of men endowed with free will.

National character undoubtedly exists. It consists, however, mostly of inclinations *how* to do things— slowly or rapidly, after long deliberation or suddenly, emotionally or with a show of reason, thoroughly or superficially. In other words, there is a national temperament. But it tells us nothing about the nature of

actual decisions—just as the fact that one man is superficial and the other thorough does not tell us which one
is more likely to commit murder. In addition to the tem-
peramental inclinations of a national or racial group
there are conscious or traditional decisions to regard a
certain type of person, a certain profession, a certain
type of conduct as socially more desirable than others.
It is this choice of a social "ideal type" which we often
call, mistakenly, "national character." But nothing
changes as often, as rapidly and as unpredictably as the
"ideal type" of a society. What was at a premium yesterday—for instance, the Yankee banker in the United
States whom all Europe long mistook for the true representative of American national character—is at a discount tomorrow. In the history of every European
country the "ideal type" has changed many times. If
there is one thing certain about Hitlerism, it is that the
Nazi leaders represent a type which never before has
been the "ideal type" of German society, neither in
background, nor in personal character, class antecedents,
profession, conduct, or belief. But that is simply saying
that Nazism is a revolution, which we know anyhow; it
tells us nothing about the character of the revolution,
its roots, or its meaning. Least of all does it tell us anything about the German national character except that
the Germans are as capable of having a revolution as
any other people.

Fundamentally those who accept the national-character explanation accept Hitler's doctrine. For there is little difference between the theorem of the inevitability and immutability of a nation's character and the theorem of the perennial and unchangeable "race." And once this is accepted the step toward the "innate" superiority of one nation or race is short. To overcome Nazism we must take our stand on the old Christian principle that in his moral character the common man is very much alike regardless of race, nationality, or color. This is not in itself an answer to Nazism—except in the field of purely individual ethics. It is not a basis of political action. For what matters in political and social life is not innate nature but ethical principles, objective reality, and the application of the first to the organization of the second: political institutions. Both, principles and reality, are quite independent of the innate nature of the common man—the first a decision of man's free will, the second a heteronomous condition. But both are equally independent of national or racial character.

If the national-character explanation is untenable, the national-history explanations are meaningless. If the Germans instead of Nazism had developed a German form of the Gandhi pacifism, we would now have many books showing the "inevitability" of this development

in the light of the Reformation, Luther, Kant, Beethoven
or F. W. Foerster; and there were a great many more
devoted pacifists in the Germany of 1927 as there were
devoted Nazis. If the English had developed a totalitarian philosophy, the pseudo historians would have had
a field day with Henry VIII, that great totalitarian
Cromwell, Hobbes, Bentham, Carlyle, Spencer, and
Bosanquet. There has been no great historical figure, no
great thinker in any country whose thoughts and deeds
cannot be construed as to lead "inevitably" and at the
same time to two diametrically opposed conclusions. A
century ago it was customary in both England and America to start every historical book with a long hymn of
praise of those Teutonic qualities which in Arminius,
Luther, and Frederick the Great shook off the yoke of
Latin tyranny and founded freedom; then the enemies
were France and Popery. Now, with Nazism the danger,
we encounter the theory that Hitler's tyranny was inevitable because the Romans never civilized Northern
Germany and because Luther destroyed the Catholic
civilization of the Middle Ages. How does this account
for the Norwegians or for the far less Romanized and
equally protestant Scotch or Dutch?

Actually, the immediate ancestors of the more striking Nazi doctrines and slogans were mostly non-
Germans. The first and the most consistent modern
totalitarian philosopher was the Frenchman Auguste

Comte—one of the most influential writers of the nineteenth century. It is significant that Comte was the first
thinker who focused on industry; and his totalitarianism, especially his hatred of free speech, free thought,
and free conscience, grew out of an attempt to organize
society around the industrial producer. Racial anti-
Semitism also comes from France where Gobineau first
pronounced it; and he in turn was the direct descendant
of a long line of French political thinkers who tried to
explain and to justify the social order of France as due
to the racial origin of the various social strata and to
the inherent superiority or inferiority of different races.
They even had the same "scientific" nonsense that Nazism uses.* The two Napoleons developed most of the
principles of foreign policy which Hitler employs; and
both had learned from Machiavelli as well as from the
shrewd power politicians of Venice and Holland. The
concept of the "Chosen People" is of course, taken directly from the Jews against whom it has been used so
brutally and fiendishly. It was the American William
James who first developed the ideas of noneconomic
hierarchies on which the Nazi party and its organizations are so largely based; it is ironical—but typical
for the way in which ideas descend—that he did so in

---

* In this field Mr. Jacques Barzun has done pioneer work; his books,
especially *The French Race* and *Race*, ought to be required reading for
all who want to understand the real nature of the pseudoscientific biological theories in current political thought.

an essay, called "The Moral Equivalent for War," which set out to establish permanent peace. It was an English admiral who laid the foundations for "Geopolitics." And it was the American War Industries Board of 1917 which first developed a modern total-war economy. To make either Gobineau, James or any of the others responsible for the use or abuse to which the Nazis have put their ideas would obviously be as ridiculous as to call the French, English, or Americans inherently and inevitably fascist because of the nationality of their various writers and statesmen. But it is just as silly to trace inevitabilities in German history. All that can be proved is the extremely close contact and the very extensive and continuous cross-fertilization of all European cultures, which make any talk of "inherent characteristics" of any one nation perfectly nonsensical.

The truth is that every nation has in its history and in its character an infinite capacity for good and for evil; that it has precedents and authorities for one line of action or for the very opposite; and that its decision is its own decision and determined neither by its nature nor by its past heritage.

The flimsiest theories of Nazism—or of any other historical phenomenon—are those which try to interpret or explain its meaning and origin as due to specific institutions, or to geographic accidents. At one time it was fondly believed that Nazism was largely the result of a long development of industrial concentration under government control. Undoubtedly the concrete details of certain Nazi institutions were formed by this development. But neighboring Czechoslovakia had a far greater degree of industrial concentration and cartelization, and a far more complete government control. Yet the Nazism that was allegedly the inevitable outcome of such a development in Germany was conspicuously absent in Czechoslovakia. And the most paternalist economic policy of modern Europe was that of France where eighteenth century mercantilism was never given up. Yet it would be ridiculous to make the French supervision of trade responsible for the "Men of Vichy."

Again, there is no doubt that Nazism marched east and conquered the little countries in eastern and southeastern Europe. But Nazism is not just the *Drang nach Osten* or the German-Slav thousand years' war. Every time that Germany wanted to expand, she had to come into conflict with the Slavonic people, simply because Slavs and not Siamese live on Germany's eastern border. And for the same reason the Slavonic people always had a *Drang nach Westen.* In other words, for a thousand years Slavs and Germany have inevitably been in very close contact, fighting each other part of the time, but also living together peaceably and learning from each other. That Germany borders on Slavonic countries does not explain the Nazi urge for conquests or for world domination. Nor do past attempts to conquer Slavonic territory explain anything about the nature of the present attempt—except that the geology and geography of central Europe is still what it was five hundred years ago.

It is very important to understand clearly that Nazism cannot be explained as due to the German national character, the German history, or the German institutional and geographic conditions. Without such realization the present war becomes meaningless and, worse still, there can be no realization of the tremendous danger of Nazism. If, indeed, as has been so often and so popularly said, the Nazi system is the result of something that is inevitable in the German national character or in German history, there would be no point in English or American participation in the war. There is no discernible American interest to prevent Germany's "historical and irreducible" desire to subjugate the Slavs. There would be no hope that these desires could ever be extinguished; for can five years of war be expected to do what five hundred years have not been able to do? On the theory of inevitability, the only conclusion would be to let the Germans have their apparently inevitable way and to be cut in on the swag. And Hitler, himself one of the leading lights of the inevitability school, apparently expected just that and based his whole policy on this argument.

Unless we realize that the essence of Nazism is the attempt to solve a universal problem of Western civilization—that of the industrial society—and that the basic principles on which the Nazis base this attempt are also in no way confined to Germany, we do not know what we fight for or what we fight against. We must know that we fight against an attempt to develop a functioning industrial society on the basis of slavery and conquest. Otherwise we would have no basis for our own attempt to develop not only a functioning but a free and peaceful industrial society. All we could hope for would be the elimination of the unimportant features of Nazism —those due either to the chances of Germany's economic position in 1933 or to the accidents of her concrete institutions. If we really imagined that we fight against the barter system of international trade or for the Rhine border, we would stake the social and political order of the Western world after this war on gambler's luck.

The very monstrosity of totalitarian tyranny is sufficient proof that the society which made possible the emergence of such a nightmare and of such a threat must have failed to discharge its elementary functions. The violent repression of freedom by the totalitarians proves that they are trying to make society function by abandoning freedom. To overcome totalitarianism we must recreate a functioning society, and one that functions at least as well as the totalitarian pseudo society. And it must be a free society. To understand the issues, to see the task, to work out the approaches to its achievement is not only essential for the winning of the peace; it is part and parcel of the winning of the war.

CHAPTER TWO

WHAT IS A FUNCTIONING
SOCIETY?

WE DO not today have a functioning industrial society. We have a magnificent technical machine for industrial production, built and run by engineers, chemists, and skilled mechanics. We have a considerably weaker but still very impressive economic machine for the distribution of industrial goods. Politically and socially, however, we have no industrial civilization, no industrial community life, no industrial order or organization. It is this absence of a functioning industrial society, able to integrate our industrial reality, which underlies the crisis of our times.

The physical reality in which live the overwhelming majority of the five hundred million people on the European and North American Continents is that of an industrial world. Few of us could live a single day without the products, services, and institutions of the industrial system. Everything in our lives which relates to the routine of living is shaped and determined by it. Most of us depend upon it directly or indirectly for our livelihood and our pleasures. Its social problems are our individual problems; its crises are direct attacks upon our individual security and our social stability; its triumphs are our proudest achievements. Western Man has become Industrial Man.

But Western society is still fundamentally preindustrial in its social beliefs and values, its social institutions and economic instruments. It is in the last analysis a mercantile society evolved at the close of the eighteenth century. This preindustrial society most successfully organized the physical reality of the nineteenth century. But it cannot integrate the industrial reality of today.

Man in his social and political existence must have a functioning society just as he must have air to breathe in his biological existence. However, the fact that man has to have a society does not necessarily mean that he has it. Nobody calls the mass of unorganized, panicky, stampeding humanity in a shipwreck a "society." There is no society, though there are human beings in a group. Actually, the panic is directly due to the breakdown of a society; and the only way to overcome it is by restoring a society with social values, social discipline, social power, and social organization.

Social life cannot function without a society; but it is conceivable that it does not function at all. The evidence of the last twenty-five years of Western civilization hardly entitles us to say that our social life functioned so well as to make out a prima facie case for the existence of a functioning society.

It is of course not true that a society must grow out of the material reality around it. There can be a social organization of a physical reality on the basis of values, disciplines, ideals, conventions and powers which belong completely to another social reality. Take, for instance, Robinson Crusoe and his man Friday. Undoubtedly they had a society. Nothing is more ridiculous than the traditional view of Robinson as the isolated individualist Economic Man. He had social values, conventions, taboos, powers, etc. His society was not one developed according to the demands of life on a subtropical islet in the southern Pacific Ocean, but basically that of Calvinist Scotsmen developed on the cold shores of the North Atlantic. What is so marvelous in Robinson Crusoe is not the extent to which he adapted himself, but the almost complete absence of adaptation. Had he been of a different class and a different time, he would surely have dressed for dinner in the evening. Here we have a case where a successful social life was built on the values and concepts of a society quite different in its physical reality and problems from those to which it was adapted.

A society may be based on concepts and beliefs developed to organize a specific physical reality. Or it may rest on foundations as alien to its surroundings as were those of Robinson Crusoe's society to San Juan Fernandez. But it must always be capable of organizing the actual reality in a social order. It must master the material world, make it meaningful and comprehensible for the individual; and it must establish legitimate social and political power.

The reality of the industrial system, though it grew out of the mercantile society and the market, was from the start different from, and often incompatible with, the basic assumptions on which the mercantile society rested. Yet during the entire nineteenth century the mercantile society succeeded in mastering, organizing, integrating the growing industrial reality. There was tension even in the early years. The history of the conflict between mercantile assumptions and industrial reality, between Jeffersonian policies and Hamiltonian facts, between the market and the system of industrial production, is very largely the social history of the hundred years before the first World War. During the closing years of the last century it became increasingly clear that the mercantile society was disintegrating, and that the industrial system was getting out of hand socially. But it was not until after 1918—maybe not until after 1929—that the mercantile society broke down. By now, however, it has ceased to be a functioning society.

2.

To define what a society is, is just as impossible as to define life. We are so close to it that the basic simple characteristics disappear behind a bewildering and complex mass of details. We are also so much part of it that we cannot possibly see the whole. And finally, there is no sharp line, no point where nonlife turns definitely into life, nonsociety definitely into society. But, although we do not know what life is, all of us know when a living body ceases to be a living body and becomes a corpse. We know that the human body cannot function as a living body if the heart has ceased to beat or the lungs stopped breathing. As long as there is a heartbeat or a breath, there is a live body; without them there is only a corpse. Similarly the impossibility of a normative definition of society does not prevent us from understanding society functionally. No society can function as a society unless it gives the individual member social status and function, and unless the decisive social power is legitimate power. The former establishes the basic frame of social life: the purpose and meaning of society. The latter shapes the space within the frame: it makes society concrete and creates its institutions. If the individual is not given social status and function, there can be no society but only a mass of social atoms flying through space without aim or purpose. And unless power is legitimate there can be no social fabric; there is only a social vacuum held together by mere slavery or inertia.

It is only natural to ask which of these criteria is more important or which of these principles of social life comes first. This question is as old as political thinking itself. It was the basis for the first sharp cleavage in political theory, that between Plato and Aristotle, between the priority of the purpose of society and that of its institutional organization. But though hallowed by antiquity and great names, it is a meaningless question. There can be no question of primacy—neither in time nor in importance—between basic political concepts and basic political institutions. Indeed, it is the very essence of political thought and action that they have always one pole in the conceptual realm of beliefs, aims, desires, and values, and one in the pragmatic realm of facts, institutions, and organization. The one without the other is not politics. The exclusively conceptual may be sound philosophy or sound ethics; the exclusively pragmatic, sound anthropology or sound journalism. Alone, neither of them can make sound politics or, indeed, politics at all.

Social status and function of the individual is the equation of the relationship between the group and the individual member. It symbolizes the integration of the individual with the group, and that of the group with the individual. It expresses the individual purpose in terms of the society, and the social purpose in terms of the individual. It thus makes comprehensible and rational individual existence from the point of the group, and group existence from that of the individual.

For the individual there is no society unless he has social status and function. Society is only meaningful if its purpose, its aims, its ideas and ideals make sense in terms of the individual's purposes, aims, ideas and ideals. There must be a definite functional relationship between individual life and group life.

This relationship might lie in an identity of purpose under which there would be no individual life other than social life, and under which the individual would have none but social aims. This was basically the position of the great Greek political philosophers, especially of Plato; and the Socratic attack against the Sophists was largely directed against an "individualist" concept of personality. The "polis" of the Socratic school is absolutely collectivist in the sense that there is no possibility of distinction between group purpose and individual purpose, group virtue and individual virtue, group life and individual life. But it is just as possible to assume no group purpose and no social life except in individual purpose and individual life—the position of the extreme, early nineteenth-century individualists.

There need not even be an assumption of identity

between individual and social purposes. Indeed, one of the most rigid of all theories of functional relationship between group and individual is the class-war theory of the Marxists which assumes a permanent conspiracy of the propertied minority against the property-less majority. Organized society in the Marxist pattern is the instrument of oppression. And to this assumption of conflict, Marxism—otherwise discredited and disproved —owed its appeal during the Depression years; it alone seemed able to explain rationally what was happening at a time when the traditional theories of harmony between individual and social purposes could not make sense at all.

For the individual without function and status, society is irrational, incalculable and shapeless. The "rootless" individual, the outcast—for absence of social function and status casts a man from the society of his fellows— sees no society. He sees only demoniac forces, half sensible, half meaningless, half in light and half in darkness, but never predictable. They decide about his life and his livelihood without possibility of interference on his part, indeed without possibility of his understanding them. He is like a blindfolded man in a strange room, playing a game of which he does not know the rules; and the prize at stake is his own happiness, his own livelihood, and even his own life.

That the individual should have social status and function is just as important for society as for him. Unless the purpose, aims, actions and motives of the individual member are integrated with the purpose, aims, actions and motives of society, society cannot understand or contain him. The asocial, uprooted, unintegrated individual appears not only as irrational but as a danger; he is a disintegrating, a threatening, a mysteriously shadowy force. It is no coincidence that so many of the great myths—the Wandering Jew, Dr. Faustus, Don Juan—are myths of the individual who has lost or repudiated social function and status. Lack of social status and function, and absence of a functional relationship between society and individual are at the bottom of every persecution of minorities which either are without social status and function—that is, not integrated into society (like the Negro in America) —or are made the scapegoat for the lack of integration in society (like the Jew in Nazi Germany).

That the individual must have definite social status in society does not mean that he must have a *fixed* social status. To identify "definite" with "frozen" was the great mistake of the early nineteenth century Liberals such as Bentham. It was a tragic misunderstanding as it led to a social atomism which repudiated social values altogether. Of course, a society may give fixed status and function to the individual. The Hindu caste system is the expression of a definite functional relationship between the group and the individual integrating them in a religious purpose. It obtains its rationality from the religious doctrine of perpetual rebirth until complete purification. On that basis even the Untouchables have a social status and function which make society and their individual life in it meaningful to them, and their life meaningful and indeed necessary to society. It is only when this religious creed itself disintegrates that the Hindu social system loses its rationality for both, individual and society.*

On the other hand, in the society of the American frontier with its complete fluidity, the individual had just as much definite social status and function as the Untouchable or the Brahmin in the Hindu society with its absolutely rigid castes. It may even be said that no society ever succeeded as perfectly in integrating its members in a functional relationship between individual and group as the frontier of Jackson, Henry Clay or Lincoln. What counts is that the status is definite, functionally understandable and purposefully rational, and not whether it is fixed, flexible or fluid. To say that every boy has an equal chance to become president is

---

* This is not, of course, saying that the Hindu social system grew out of the Hindu religion. It would be just as compatible with my argument if Hinduism had been "invented" as a rationalization of a system of graduated slavery imposed by a conqueror. Ours is a purely functional analysis and not a philosophy of history.

just as much a definition of a functional relationship between group and individual as to say that the individual is born only that he may try to escape being reborn in the same caste.

It will be clear from the foregoing that the type and form of the functional relationship between society and individual in any given society depends upon the basic belief of this society regarding the nature and fulfillment of man. The nature of man may be seen as free or unfree, equal or unequal, good or evil, perfect, perfectible or imperfect. The fulfillment may be seen in this world or in the next; in immortality or in the final extinction of the individual soul which the religions of the East preach; in peace or in war; in economic success or in a large family. The belief regarding the nature of man determines the purpose of society; the belief regarding his fulfillment, the sphere in which realization of the purpose is sought.

Any one of these basic beliefs about the nature and fulfillment of man will lead to a different society and a different basic functional relationship between society and the individual. Which of these beliefs is the right one, which is true or false, good or evil, Christian or anti-Christian, does not occupy us here. The point is that any one of these beliefs can be the basis for a working and workable society; that is, for one in which the individual has social status and function. And conversely, any society, regardless of the nature of its basic beliefs, can work only as long as it gives the individual a social status and function.

Legitimate power stems from the same basic belief of society regarding man's nature and fulfillment on which the individual's social status and function rest. Indeed, legitimate power can be defined as rulership which finds its justification in the basic ethos of the society. In every society there are many powers which have nothing to do with such a basic principle, and institutions which in no way are either designed or devoted to its fulfillment. In other words, there are always a great many "unfree" institutions in a free society, a great many inequalities in an equal society, and a great many sinners among the saints. But as long as that decisive social power which we call rulership is based upon the claim of freedom, equality or saintliness, and is exercised through institutions which are designed toward the fulfillment of these ideal purposes, society can function as a free, equal or saintly society. For its institutional structure is one of legitimate power.

This does not mean that it is immaterial whether nondecisive powers and institutions of a society are in contradiction to its basic principles. On the contrary, the most serious problems of politics arise from such conflicts. And a society may well feel that a nondecisive institution or power relationship is in such blatant contrast to its basic beliefs as to endanger social life in spite of its nondecisive character. The best case in point is that of the American Civil War when the chattel-slavery of the South was felt to endanger the whole structure of a free society. Yet the decisive power of ante-bellum America was undoubtedly legitimate power deriving its claim from the principle of freedom, and exercised through institutions designed and devoted to the realization of freedom. American society did thus function as a free society. It was indeed only because it functioned as such that it felt slavery as a threat.

What is the decisive power, and the decisive institutional organization in any society cannot be determined by statistical analysis.

Nothing could be more futile than to measure a society by counting noses, quoting tax receipts or comparing income levels. Decisive is a political, and that means a purely qualitative, term. The English landed gentry comprised never more than a small fraction of the population; furthermore, after the rise of the merchants and manufacturers it had only a very modest share of the national wealth and income. Nevertheless, down to our times it held the decisive social power. Its institutions were the decisive institutions of English society. Its beliefs were the basis for social life; its standards the representative standards; its way of life the social pattern. And its personality ideal, the gentleman, remained the ideal type of all society. Its power was not only decisive; it was legitimate power.

Equally, laws and constitutions will rarely, if ever, tell us where the decisive power lies. In other words, rulership is not identical with political government. Rulership is a social, political government largely a legal category. The Prussian Army between 1870 and 1914 was, for instance, hardly as much as mentioned in the Imperial German Constitution; yet it undoubtedly held decisive power and probably legitimately. The government was actually subordinated to the army, in spite of a civilian and usually antimilitaristic Parliament.

Another example is that of British "indirect rule" in certain African colonies. There the socially decisive power is within the tribes. At least in theory the government of the white man wields no social power at all; it confines itself to mere police matters designed to support and to maintain the social organization of the tribes within a loose and purely normative framework of "law and order." Yet, constitutionally, the governor and his council have absolute power.

Finally, it should be understood that legitimacy is a purely functional concept. There is no absolute legitimacy. Power can be legitimate only in relation to a basic social belief. What constitutes "legitimacy" is a question that must be answered in terms of a given society and its given political beliefs. Legitimate is a power when it is justified by an ethical or metaphysical principle that has been accepted by the society. Whether this principle is good or bad ethically, true or false metaphysically, has nothing to do with legitimacy which is as indifferent ethically and metaphysically as any other formal criterion. Legitimate power is socially functioning power; but why it functions and to what purpose is a question entirely outside and before legitimacy.

Failure to understand this was responsible for the confusion which made "legitimism" the name of a political creed in the early nineteenth century. The European reactionaries of 1815 were, of course, absolutely within their rights when they taught that no society could be *good* except under an absolute monarch; to have an opinion on what is desirable or just as basis of a society is not only a right, it is a duty, of man. But they were simply confusing ethical choice with functional analysis, when they said that no society could *function* unless it had an absolute monarch. And they were provably wrong when they proclaimed the dogma that only absolute monarchy was *legitimate*. Actually, after the Napoleonic Wars, absolute monarchy was illegitimate in Europe; the dynastic principle had ceased to be a legitimate claim to decisive power. The revolutionary half century before 1815 had resulted in a change in basic beliefs which made illegitimate any but constitutionally limited government. This change may have been desirable or deplorable; but it was a fact. The Legitimists might have tried to make undone this change in beliefs. They might have maintained that it would be better for the individual and for society to have an illegitimate absolute rule than a legitimate constitutional one. Or they might have invoked a "right of resistance," of secession or of revolution. The only basis on which their claim could not be based politically was that of legitimacy.

The functional analysis as to what is legitimate power does not in any way prejudge the ethical question of the individual's right or duty to resist what he considers pernicious power. Whether it is better that society perish than that justice perish is a question outside and before functional analysis. The same man who maintains most vigorously that society can function only under a legitimate power may well decide that society is less of a value than certain individual rights or beliefs. But he cannot decide, as the Legitimists did, that his values and beliefs *are* the socially accepted values and beliefs because they *ought* to be.

Illegitimate power is a power which does not derive its claim from the basic beliefs of the society. Accordingly, there is no possibility to decide whether the ruler wielding the power is exercising it in conformity with the purpose of power or not; for there is no social purpose. Illegitimate power cannot be controlled; it is by its nature uncontrollable. It cannot be made responsible since there is no criterion of responsibility, no socially accepted final authority for its justification. And what is unjustifiable cannot be responsible.

For the same reason, it cannot be limited. To limit the exercise of power is to fix the lines beyond which power ceases to be legitimate; that is, ceases to realize the basic social purpose. And if power is not legitimate to begin with, there are no limits beyond which it ceases to be legitimate.

No illegitimate ruler can possibly be a good or wise ruler. Illegitimate power invariably corrupts; for it can be only "might," never authority. It cannot be a controlled, limited, responsible, or rationally determinable power. And it has been an axiom of politics—ever since Tacitus in his history of the Roman emperors gave us one case study after another—that no human being, however good, wise or judicious, can wield uncontrolled, irresponsible, unlimited or rationally not determinable power without becoming very soon arbitrary, cruel, inhuman and capricious—in other words, a tyrant.

For all these reasons a society in which the socially decisive power is illegitimate power cannot function as a society. It can only be held together by sheer brute force—tyranny, slavery, civil war. Of course, force is the ultimate safeguard of every power; but in a functioning society it is not more than a desperate remedy for exceptional and rare diseases. In a functioning society power is exercised as authority, and *authority is the rule of right over might.* But only a legitimate power can have authority and can expect and command that social self-discipline which alone makes organized institutional life possible. Illegitimate power, even if wielded by the best and the wisest, can never depend upon anything but the submission to force. On that basis a functioning, institutional organization of social life cannot be built. Even the best tyrant is still a tyrant.

What have we proved so far? That a society cannot function unless it gives the individual member social status and function, and unless its socially decisive power is legitimate power. This may be called a "pure theory of society." Like all "pure theories" it is exclusively formal. It says nothing about the contents of a society, about freedom, religion, equality, justice, individual rights, progress, peacefulness and all the other values of social life. And to think, as a great many social efficiency engineers think today, that functioning is all that matters in social life is a complete misunderstanding of the limits and the importance of sheer efficiency. In itself functional efficiency is nothing unless we know the answer to the question: efficiency to what purpose and at what price?

I cannot dissociate myself sharply enough from the relativists to whom every society appears equally good, provided it functions. But I am just as opposed to the extremists on the other side who brush aside all questions of function and efficiency, and who refuse to consider anything but basic beliefs and ideas. It seems to me not only that this group—we might call them the Absolutists—refuse to see that basic values can only be effective in a functioning society. They also refuse to see that there is only one alternative to a functioning society: the dissolution of society into anarchic masses.

Perhaps the greatest fallacy of our age is the myth of the masses which glorifies the amorphous, society-less, disintegrated crowd. Actually, the masses are a product of social decomposition and a rank poison.

The danger does not lie in a "revolt of the masses" as Mr. Ortega y Gasset thought. Revolt is, after all, still a form of participation in social life, if only in protest. The masses are completely incapable of any active social participation which presupposes social values and an organization of society. The danger of the masses lies precisely in this inability to participate, in their apathy, cynical indifference, and complete despair. Since they have no social status and function, society to them is nothing but a demoniac, irrational, incomprehensible threat. Since they have no basic beliefs which could serve as basis for legitimate power, any legitimate authority appears to them as tyrannical and arbitrary. They are therefore always willing to follow an irrational appeal, or to submit to an arbitrary tyrant if only he promises a change. As social outcasts the masses have nothing to lose—not even their chains. Being amorphous, they have no structure of their own which would resist an arbitrary tyrannical attempt to shape them. Without beliefs, they can swallow anything provided it is not a social order. In other words, the masses must always fall prey to the demagogue or the tyrant who seeks power for power's sake. They can only be organized by force, in slavery and in negation. And they must be thus organized unless they can be reintegrated into a functioning society. Any society which cannot prevent the development of masses is doomed. That it is the fault of the society which fails to integrate its members rather than that of the masses, which are the unwilling product of social failure, does not change the pernicious character of the amorphous, basically anarchic masses.

CHAPTER THREE

THE MERCANTILE SOCIETY OF THE NINETEENTH CENTURY

THE Western world in the 150 years before the last war undoubtedly had a functioning society—a society which integrated its members in a common social purpose, and which was ruled by legitimate power. It was not only a functioning, it was a free, society; and no society can possibly be free unless it functions. But in every respect the nineteenth-century society was not an industrial society. Though it actually succeeded in mastering an ever-growing industrial reality, it was never intended and never organized for such a task. In origin, aims, beliefs and institutions, the nineteenth-century society was preindustrial, if not anti-industrial.

Although our civilization became increasingly one of industrial cities during the nineteenth century, our social forms remained those of a rural society supporting and surrounding trading towns. It was a mercantile society—commercial yet still rural. We actually tried to shut out the industrial reality from our social lives. It appeared to us as sordid, as unrefined and as something which must be kept rigorously away from our real values. That so many city children have never seen a cow is generally regarded as a scandal—and rightly so. But that a great many more—especially in Europe— have never been inside a factory should have been even more astounding. Actually, all of us accepted it as the most natural thing in the world, precisely because the industrial system was not part of the social order in which we lived.

The situation showed most clearly in England. And England, up to 1914, was the representative country which served as a model for the social organization and the social ideals of all Europe. She was the most thoroughly industrialized country in which agriculture had all but disappeared. Yet England was also the country in which the mercantile society was entrenched most strongly and developed most successfully. The "gentleman," the social ideal which dominated England in the nineteenth century, could be defined as someone who is not connected with the industrial system and who lives in a preindustrial order. It is typical that the concession which society made to the rising urban middle classes was the inclusion of the professions and of the merchants in the class of gentlemen. Surgeons and lawyers became gentlemen; and so did export merchants, stock and commodity brokers, bankers, wholesalers, insurance brokers and ship owners. But manufacturing never became a gentlemanly profession. As late as 1935 young men would prefer a junior partnership in a small insurance broker firm to a much better paid executive job in a manufacturing corporation with the argument that "the City is at least a proper place for a gentleman."

In its social life England had but one ideal type and social pattern—that of the rural gentry. This ideal was not just proclaimed by the upper classes. It was accepted and affirmed by the small clerks and the industrial workers. It formed their idea of society, molded their standards of conduct and propriety, and served as the fixed star by which they oriented themselves and determined their social position. There simply was no social life, no community, no organization of the industrial world. It is no accident that the countless novels produced in England since 1830 all deal with life in the country or in London. Only Arnold Bennett, as far as I know, described life in the industrial towns in which the majority of English people live.

Disraeli almost a hundred years ago spoke of the "Two Nations" in England, the rural-commercial and the industrial. Actually, up to our time the second of these two had never been integrated into society. The huge smoking industrial cities of the Midlands and of the North were politically more important in 1938 than had been the industrial villages of 1838, when England was still largely a mercantile country. But socially and

culturally, the industrial towns were still on the periphery. The basis of social rule had broadened; more
people were counted "gentlemen." Trade no longer disqualified, and some trades had actually become endowed
with social prestige. The foxhunting squire seemed ridiculous to a good many people—though mostly to people of his own class. But the social beliefs and ideals of
England, the standards of conduct, the ways of living,
the scale of individual and social ambitions had hardly
changed since England's greatest social analyst, Jane
Austen, portrayed the generation of 1800 when the merchant first became a gentleman, and when manufacturer
and industrial worker were still so unusual as to go
unmentioned.

Up to our present time the industrial groups—both
workers and employers—seemed to be content to have
the gentry in command. They seemed to expect leadership and responsibility from the Gentleman. In any real
crisis they turned to him—certainly up to 1914 and
largely even to 1940. It was not until the general strike
of 1926 that Transport House (the trade-union head-
quarters) and the British Iron and Steel Federation
began to intervene directly into politics.

The leadership which the gentry gave, the responsibilities which they assumed, the political wisdom which
they had accumulated, were indeed of a high order.
Nothing is less intelligent than the propaganda attempts

to show up the squirarchy and the "Old School Tie" as a bunch of reactionary usurpers. While suffering from stupidity, greed, shortsightedness and lust of power as much as every other ruling class in history, they had unusual political instinct and responsibility. They also represented truly and faithfully the mercantile ideals and beliefs which industrialized England cherished. It will be hard to find any group as good as, or better than, they were. The first experiments with leaders representing industrial values and industrial beliefs: MacDonald, Baldwin, Neville Chamberlain, have not been too encouraging. With all his many virtues—and his vices— the Gentleman who ruled and represented England up to this war was the social type of a preindustrial, mercantile society, had preindustrial mercantile ideals and beliefs, and derived his claim to power from the purposes and concepts of a preindustrial half-rural, half-commercial society.

On the Continent of Europe the social order and political organization of the 150 years before 1918 was not only preindustrial but anti-industrial.

Up to the present war France had a social ideal which was as firmly entrenched as was the Gentleman across the Channel: the ideal of the "peasant proprietor." The independent, basically self-sufficient farm entrepreneur on his own land was the ideal type of French society from Robespierre to Pétain. All the great men of France's political and social life from the fall of Napoleon onward have come from this class, have spoken its language and shared its beliefs. They have all looked forward to retirement as small but independent farmers as the one fitting reward of a successful life. Their attitude was shared by the other members of the middle class who were forced to make their living in the cities as *fonctionnaires*, as clerks, shopkeepers, lawyers or doctors. The goal of their ambitions was to save up enough to retire to a small farm of their own as soon as possible, there to live modestly, independently, and in leisure.

It was popularly believed during the Depression of the thirties that industrial unemployment was no real problem in France because most of the unemployed could go home to a farm. There was very little truth in this thesis. But its almost universal acceptance in France and abroad shows vividly the kind of society Frenchmen wanted to live in. The French way of life was at once the most bourgeois and the most anti-industrial in all Western Europe. It represented most clearly the conviction of the late eighteenth century that its mercantile society—rural yet commercial—was the fulfillment of the ages and the apogee of creation. And it was least capable of all the social beliefs of nineteenth-century industrial Europe to organize an industrial system. It was the consistency, the balance, the dignity and humanism of her social ideal which gave to the France of yesterday her attraction. But the same qualities also are responsible for the complete failure of the country to integrate industry, to give social status and function to the industrial worker, or to have any but despotic power in the industrial system. Before 1914 this was perhaps a minor problem as the social reality of France corresponded largely to the mercantilist assumptions. With the tremendous expansion of modern industry in France after 1918, the conflict between mercantilist beliefs and industrial reality became, however, unbearable.

To the French bourgeois proprietor, industry appeared as an abomination and as the denial of all he believed in. Convinced that there can be no human dignity and human virtue without a stake in property, he feared and hated the industrial worker as inherently undignified and evil. No other country had as deep and as profound a feeling of class hatred as had France. In no other country was there as little social contact between the prevailing society and the industrial worker. The industrial suburbs of Paris, or the bleak misery of the Borinage, the mining district on the Franco-Belgian border, were separated from society as if by an invisible quarantine. Half ghettos, half besieged fortresses, they were kept under rigorous watch by the surrounding bourgeoisie which finally seemed to decide that even conquest by an alien enemy was preferable to the giving of responsibility and social status to the members of the industrial system.

The industrial employer was as little integrated into French society as the industrial worker. Though powerful, well-organized and envied, the industrial manager in France remained a mysterious and rather suspect person to the average Frenchman. To the bourgeois, the process of industrial production appeared as black magic—utterly incomprehensible and rather terrifying. This showed clearly in the attitude of the French middle class toward investments. The shrewdest, most careful, most businesslike *proprietaire* could never distinguish between out-and-out swindles and sound industrial enterprises. He usually invested as if there were no differences between a share in a sugar refinery established a hundred years ago and firmly entrenched in its field, and a share in a scheme to build ice rinks in the center of the Sahara. The simple industrial process of sugar refining was in itself so mysterious to him as to be completely irrational and fantastic.

There were many other signs of the basically preindustrial and anti-industrial basis of French society. A characteristic though not an important one is that the great technical school of France was a school for highway and bridge building—the two branches of engineering developed and most cherished by the preindustrial

society of the eighteenth century. There was no awareness that industry was real, and accordingly none that
the industrial employer had any power. Even the Popular Front of 1935-37, nominally a government of industrial labor, attacked not the power of the industrial
employers but the bogeyman of the "Hundred Families"
—the great merchant and banking families of 1848
whose power had actually been transferred after 1918
to the industrial managers and their trade associations.

French society understood industry in the terms of
the eighteenth century. A plant with ten thousand workers was regarded as only an enlarged version of the
artisan's workshop with its three journeymen and four
apprentices. Society refused to see that the manager of
the modern plant is not just a master-tailor or shoe-
maker. It could not understand the need of defining the
manager's power; at the same time it resented his power
as usurpation. In no other country was industrial management so despotic and, at the same time, so uneasy
as in France between the two wars.

The real social and political decisions were rapidly
pushed into the managers' laps by the tremendous industrial expansion of the country after 1918. At the same
time his power remained without roots, and it was in
open and direct contradiction to the values and beliefs
of the whole country. The social and spiritual crisis of
our times was nowhere more obvious than in the France

of the early thirties which lived in a revolutionary climate apparently far more threatening than that which led to actual revolution east of the Rhine.

In Prussia—and more or less throughout Germany—the situation was different from that of England or France in one important respect: Prussia never succeeded in developing a unified mercantile society. Culturally and socially the ideal social type and the prevailing social order were those of the mercantile society; the representative groups were the bourgeois classes of professional men, university teachers, the civil service, merchants and bankers. But the political power was in the hands of the Junkers who were anti-mercantile.

In origin, economic status, and social beliefs, the Junkers were a rural upper middle class, very much like the squires in England. Nothing is further from the truth than to regard the poor, rigidly Lutheran Junker as a nobleman, just because he has a "von" in front of his name. With his dependence upon his salary as an officer, and his ambition to reach the rank of major, the Junker was as much a product of the Commercial Revolution of the seventeenth and eighteenth centuries as the landed gentry in England or the peasant proprietor in France. He depended economically upon the sale of his services to the state and the sale of his crops to the city

Socially he was a creation of the centralized state. And standing army, city and centralized state are all products not of feudalism but of its destruction. Though bourgeois, the mentality of the Junker was antimercantilistic. He was poor; he was Lutheran and convinced of the danger of Mammon; above all, he was a professional soldier and thus not willing to accept individual self-interest as a guiding rule of moral conduct.

The antagonism between the Junker and the liberal urban middle class had most serious consequences for German development. It defeated the attempt of the great Prussian reformers of the Napoleonic era, Stein, Scharnhorst and Gneisenau, to create a successful and unified mercantile society in nineteenth-century Prussia. It created a basic split in the social personality of Germany—the truth behind all the pretentious nonsense of the "two Germanies" or of "Germany, Dr. Jekyll and Mr. Hyde." Finally, it was in part responsible for the Conservative illusion that Hitler—because he too opposed the liberal bourgeoisie—would turn out a Conservative.

The conflict within the preindustrial society gave the German industrial producer—both employer and worker—more prominence and prestige than he had in either France or England. Superficially, Germany in the nineteenth century seemed to have come closer to a solution than either England or France. The social legislation initiated by the Junkers in the 1880's to give the worker some social security seemed at first to offer a way to a real integration. The close financial ties between banks and industry in Germany seemed to make possible a unified national economy. Actually, the disintegration was worse than in the west. For the preindustrial society which was unified and functioning in the west was split and disorganized in Germany, so that it broke down under a strain which in the west was still socially bearable.

Conditions in the United States were radically different from those in industrial Europe. At first glance it might appear that in this country society succeeded in becoming an industrial society. There is little of the basic conflict between town and country which has been so prominent on the European Continent. Neither is there a preindustrial ruling class as in England. But though there is simply no basis of comparison between America and Europe, in the United States too the values, beliefs, and order of the prevailing society were those of a preindustrial society. And there has not as yet developed a functioning industrial society. By and large the old saying is true, that this country has had a Jeffersonian social creed and a Hamiltonian reality. The Free Farmer, the independent responsible citizen on his own soil, has been the representative type of American social

and political ideals. But modern mass-production industry has become the representative social reality.

The preindustrial character of American social beliefs and ideals shows in the central importance of the
"frontier" in American political thinking. It explains
the popularity of the dangerous fallacy that our basic
social and political institutions are threatened because
there is no more free land. The frontier of independent
free farmers on new land was perhaps the most consistent—certainly the most successful—of the great social ideals of a mercantile-commercial, yet rural,
society. It was not only preindustrial; in its repudiation
of any functional organization of society it was directly
anti-industrial.

The preindustrial character of American society
shows also in the pattern of the typical American success
story—typical in fiction and fact—which starts with a
boyhood on a poor New England or Kansas farm; the
"log cabin" cliché of presidential campaigns is only one
conventionalized version of this great American legend.
It shows in the fact that the one political body the bulk
of which is elected by the farm vote—the Senate—has
become the most respected of all elective bodies and the
one regarded as most truly representative of the country as a whole. The traditional belief that only recent
immigrants are unskilled workers, and that the native
American can always become independent outside of

the industrial system—as farmer, as shopkeeper, as professional man—reflects the same basic preindustrialism of society. And the Old South had its conscious anti-industrialism and its remnants of a preindustrial rural and hereditary ruling class.

The tremendous enthusiasm for mechanics in the United States might, of course, be a sign that this country is much closer to a solution than Europe. But mechanical and technical genius is not a social solution in itself. Industry is as respectable, exciting and close to the typical American as it has been hostile, remote and suspect to the representative groups in the Europe of yesterday. But the values and beliefs of this country are values and beliefs of a society in which there were no large corporations, no mass production, no permanent working class, no management power. At heart, the average American is a Populist; and the essence of Populism today consists of a refusal to admit as valid the reality of the industrial system.

2.

The mercantile society gave social function and status to the individual through his integration in the market. And its socially decisive rule was the legitimate power in the market.

The market has usually been regarded as an exclusively *economic* institution. Actually, it was the central *social* institution of the nineteenth century. In and through the market the nineteenth century mastered physical reality. In and through the market it expressed its basic beliefs and its aims. The nineteenth century saw the nature of man as "Economic Man"; it saw the aim of society as the establishment of freedom and justice through economic development. Accordingly, the individual participated in society through the exercise of his individual property rights. And they were also the basis for the legitimate power in the market.

Property has always been of vital importance in social life. It has always been one source of social prestige and political power. It may even have been a good deal more important to the individual in the twelfth century, when goods were very scarce and the differences in wealth between rich and poor very great, than in the nineteenth century when goods became more plentiful in the western world and economic differences leveled off markedly. Certainly the individual became far less mercenary as the earning of a sustenance became easier. One need only read Jane Austen and compare her English upper middle class of 1800 with the same class a hundred years later, to see that during the mercantile century the lust for wealth and money became steadily less prominent as a motive of individual behavior. The people in whose lives and dreams the desire to own property loomed largest were the groups most remote from, and most inimical to, the market: land-starved Irish or Balkan peasants.

The familiar charge that the mercantile society with its "commercialism" degraded men into money-grabbing hogs is totally unfounded. What is more important: It is a confusion between individual behavior and social structure.

The mercantile society did not make man more interested in economic wealth. It did not change human nature. Indeed, no society could possibly change human nature. Man will always strive for economic success in his economic life, just as he will strive for success in all other fields of life. After Economic Man has disappeared as a social ideal, people in their economic life will still want economic gain; the banker of the future —or whoever will fulfill the functions of credit-broker —will be in business for profit or for the rewards of management, and not "for his health." Different men will give different values to different rewards in different fields of endeavor. There exist apparently basic human types who find their individual satisfaction in different activities. It is probable that both the types and their respective shares in the total population have remained largely unchanged through history, and that they are very much the same all the world over.

But all this has little or nothing to do with society.

Socially the mercantile society gave an entirely new meaning to property. In the past, property had always been regarded as an effect of the social order. Men had title to property because they had a certain social status; or they obtained property as an aftereffect of their achievement in a socially prominent sphere. Property was an appurtenance to social status and function. But the mercantile society saw property as the *cause* of social status. It saw in the exercise of individual property rights the social function of the individual. It made economic rewards the socially significant rewards, economic prestige the socially decisive prestige, economic activity the representative activity of the society.

Statistically, just as many people may have striven primarily for economic gain in the nineteenth century as in earlier societies; and as many may have sought their satisfactions outside of the market. However, society is not a matter of statistics but of emphasis. What counts are not numbers but the principles and beliefs on which the statistics are selected and organized. What decides the nature of a society is not the prevailing but the representative social sphere. And the emphasis, the principle of selection and organization, the representative social sphere of the mercantile society, were all focused on economic activity, based on individual property rights and expressed through the market.

Property rights as such did not change. But their

social meaning and consequences did. Locke's statement in the closing years of the seventeenth century that a thing becomes a man's property because he has commingled his labor with it, represented a radically new and revolutionary concept of property as basis of society and as justification of social power. Property had been fixed as the object of human action and of social rights. It now became the vehicle of social action. This is what Sir Henry Maine meant by his famous epigram that history had moved from status to contract. Formerly, Maine said, the status was fixed as between man and man from which followed a relationship between man and property. Now it is the relationship between property and property—the essence of a contract—which determines the status between men who have no other social relationship. It is through property, in other words, that the individual is integrated in the group.

This new concept of property meant that the entire economic sphere had to be subject to the market. Everything had to be capable of becoming property. Hence the insistence of the market system that the basic factors of economic life be regarded and treated as commodities: land, labor, money. The claim that there is a difference in kind between land and other property, or between labor and other property, could not be allowed. It would have caused a need for social integration outside of the market; and such a claim would have been a denial of Economic Man. The worker must be regarded as someone who has a property in the commodity called labor—which is in no way different from property in anything else. For then he can be conceived as capable of social activity in the market through which he fulfills his nature as Economic Man, and in and through which he has status and function in society.

Most important, yet least understood, is the organization of decisive social power in the market. According to the textbooks—even to those few which recognize the function of property as the basis of legitimate social power in nineteenth-century society—there was no rule in the socio-economic sphere of the mercantile society. Absence of rule in economics is traditionally regarded as the characteristic feature of "laissez faire." But this belief is only tenable—and indeed only meaningful—if rule is defined in the narrowest sense as meaning the political sovereign. On any other definition the traditional belief is simply not true. The many writers who maintain that the economic sphere is far too important to be left without rule and that it requires a government are perfectly right. They are wrong only if they think that they have disproved laissez faire or attacked the mercantile society. They either attack a bogeyman of their own creation: the "anarchic market"; or they attack the political principles of the separation of political government from rule in the socially decisive sphere on which nineteenth-century freedom largely rested.

There never was an "anarchic market" without rule and duly constituted authorities. Laissez faire only meant that the political government was to be confined to the narrowly political sphere and was not a legitimate government outside of it. But the market had a legitimate power of its own. It had rules and authority though they were not the rules and authority of the government of the political sphere. The rulers in the economic sphere were as much motivated by power considerations as the government in the political sphere. They played politics fully as much as Parliament or Congress. Only the motives, objectives and instruments of their activities were different from, and independent of, those of the political sphere proper. In short, laissez faire was nothing but a command to the government of the political sphere to observe a functional division of spheres and rules. Not only was it not opposed to a rule of the market; it required the development of such a rule.

The market was not only protected against the political government by the theoretical demands of laissez faire. It developed its own political institutions to keep the political government out. Among them the most important and powerful was the international gold standard.

The gold standard subordinated money and credit to the dictates of the most perfect market: international trade.

Economically, the subordination of domestic business to the foreign-trade balance could hardly be justified, once industry had grown beyond its first infancy. Only in England was foreign trade important enough for the economy to warrant its primacy. But even in England the industrial system might have functioned better economically if there had been no such direct link between foreign trade and domestic credit and interest rates. The experience after 1931 when this link was cut with the abolition of the gold standard disproves the traditional justification of the gold standard. For countries like the United States, where foreign trade was only marginal as far as industry was concerned, the gold standard was economically probably more of a burden than an asset.

But it is altogether a mistake to discuss the gold standard in terms of economic efficiency. It was above all a political institution—the means to establish the supremacy of the market over the industrial system and to maintain the juxtaposition of political government and society, and with it the political freedom of the mercantile society. With money and credit automatically determined by the flow of the market, the power to create credit was withheld from the government. The gold standard was a constitutional barrier to the power and sphere of the political government. What was important was not only that it made the market supreme over the industrial system, but also that it prevented the encroachment of the political government on the industrial system.

Even after the attempt to subordinate the industrial system to the market through the gold standard had proved futile, the gold standard at least guaranteed that the industrial sphere would remain a no man's land—a buffer state between the society of the market and the political government of majority rule. The conquest of this buffer state by the government after 1918 and especially after 1931, signified more than anything else in the sphere of economic institutions the collapse of the market as a society. The development of dynamic credit policies since 1918—beginning with the "Open Market" policy of the American Federal Reserve System—was perhaps the most decisive step in the breaking down of the juxtaposition of government and market on which the mercantile society had been based. The subordination of money and credit to industrial production which is so prominent in all present war economies is thus a fundamental and decisive change.

3.

It was England which developed the market to perfection. And it was her role as the most perfect mercantile society which gave England in the nineteenth century
her social, economic and cultural leadership, and which
made her the representative country of the nineteenth
century. But anyone who has ever been in business in
England knows that there was a rule in the socio-
economic sphere, and that the automatism of individual
self-interests was a myth. As late as the early and middle thirties—when I myself worked in the City of
London in the supposedly "freest" of all businesses,
international banking—the old mercantile government
of the market was still functioning. Though it had lost
considerably and was only a shadow of what it had been
twenty-five or fifty years before, it was still an extremely
powerful, immediate, and ruthless rule. Nobody in mercantile business—banker, stockbroker, wholesaler or
insurance broker—could afford to disregard it. To brush
aside an order from the duly constituted authorities of
the market meant rapid punishment. Permanent and
willful contravention of these orders or of the codes
administered by the rulers was impossible, even for
the financial or commercial giants. The penalty would
have been the destruction of the business of the offender.
Execution of such an economic death sentence pro-

nounced by the rulers would have been swift, merciless, and unappealable.

The market rulers exercised their powers through the typical institutions of the market: the central bank, the Stock Exchange, the money market, the Commodity Exchanges, the foreign exchange market, the freight exchange, etc. They ruled in the interest of the market; that is, for the political purpose of keeping the mercantile society functioning. It was the badge of statesmanship in the market to be known for putting the functioning of the market above one's own economic interests. It corresponded to the prestige which placing the interests of one's country above one's own political advancement gives in the political system. Finally, the coercion of the market government was exercised through the power of the rulers to grant or to deny access to, and membership in, the market. If, for instance, the Bank of England— the most powerful and most typical of all the mercantile rulers—wanted foreign exchange speculation to be curtailed, it did not issue an ordinance. That would have been quite contrary to the constitution of a market. It simply passed the word along. Apparently informally the hint was conveyed—over the luncheon table, in a chat over the telephone, on the Stock Exchange, or through the Foreign Exchange brokers. Nobody, at least not until the whole market structure began to disintegrate after the last war, was formally requested to cut down his dealings in foreign exchange. The offender was neither hauled into court nor fined. If he disregarded the hint—followed up perhaps with an equally discreet warning—he would suddenly find his credit curtailed or stopped; his "name" would cease to be "good delivery" on the Stock Exchange, his endorsement on a bill of exchange would no longer be accepted as "bankable signature" on the money market. His physical person would remain untouched. But the social rights to which his individual property entitled him— namely, the access to, and the equal membership in, the market—would be withdrawn.

This government of the economic sphere in the mercantile society was the same government that has ruled every commercial system: a commercial oligarchy. In their power, their composition, their code and their aims there was little difference between the legitimate rulers in the economic sphere of nineteenth-century England, America or Germany, and the commercial aristocracy of the fifteenth-century commercial cities—Venice, Florence, the Hanseatic League, or sixteenth-century Antwerp. Constitutional law could not have defined who the rulers were and how they became rulers. In this respect the City of London in 1850 differed little from the Venice of 1450. But everybody in business in nineteenth-century London, New York, Boston, Amsterdam, Hamburg or Paris knew precisely who "belonged" and who did not, who mattered and who was of no account, why one house was powerful and the other one only rich, why a hint from one was an order, and an order from another was meaningless. The qualifications for ruler-ship were as undefinable as they were well known and understood. Wealth alone was not enough; actually, the wealthiest houses in the commercial oligarchy often did not "belong." It was equally not just name and tradition. It was certainly not the greatest proficiency in business; on the contrary, "keenness" or "sharpness" disqualified one almost automatically. It was a mixture of wealth and experience, tradition and shrewdness, business acu-men and a knowledge of the invisible limitations of the unwritten code, responsibility, probity and initiative—an intangible but concrete qualification which can only be described with the word "standing." What promoted a member of the commercial system into the ranks of the rulers was tacit approval of the community and equally tacit co-option by the oligarchy. The forms in which such promotion was expressed might be an invi-tation to participate in a bond issue, election to the board of governors of the Bank of England—or simply an invitation to a card party or to membership in a breakfast club. The meaning of each of these apparently formless forms was perfectly understood by the whole community. In the society described by Jane Austen, Thackeray, or Edith Wharton the ruling oligarchy was clearly outlined; but it would have been impossible to say what these limits were. Such a structure of rulership is not only typical of an oligarchy. It is also inevitable in a market which requires both absolute elasticity and, at the same time, absolute discipline.

In fine, the great systems of the late eighteenth century did not create a functioning industrial society. Actually, they did not even see the emergence of industry.

Only one of that great generation as much as noticed industry: Hamilton. He not only saw the industrial revolution; he understood its significance. His life was almost contemporaneous with the great inventions. He reached his peak fully forty years after Watt invented the steam engine, and he died only twenty years before the emergence of the steam locomotive. Yet none of his contemporaries realized that behind Hamilton's insistence upon a strong central government and his distrust of the masses there was a tremendous vision of a revolutionary process of industrialization just ahead. To an unbiased reader today—whether he shares Hamilton's political convictions or not—the Report on Manufacture and the various financial and banking proposals made by Hamilton as Secretary of the Treasury must appear prophetic. To his contemporaries they were only attempts of a Tory to establish a monarchy over free farmers. That industrialization mattered—the basis of all Hamilton's political thought—nobody understood.

This blindness is all the more remarkable because among the contemporaries were many men of insight and genius. Jefferson, Madison, Taylor of Caroline, John Adams, were political thinkers of the highest order and of great originality. Their understanding of social forces and of political institutions has never been surpassed in this or in any other country. Yet they all thought exclusively in terms of a mercantile society. Their main economic problem was the relationship between the agrarian producer and the commercial distributor. They did not realize that right under their very eyes a new social world was rapidly coming into existence with its own social relations and political powers—the industrial system. In the few instances in which they mentioned industry, it was with contempt and aversion. There was no place for industry in their minds and in their thoughts; it was hostile to their beliefs, their institutions, and their values.

This inability to see and to comprehend the Industrial Revolution of their own time was by no means peculiar to Americans. Contemporary Europe was just as little aware of the meaning of the new forces which got their start just when the old ones were being finally organized. Adam Smith discussed industrial production; but he was most contemptuous of it and allotted to it absolutely no importance and no future. Burke, the father of England's free society in the nineteenth century, hardly ever mentioned industrial production in his social and economic works. The same is true of the philosophers and theorists of the French Revolution. Stein in Prussia had himself managed large-scale industrial enterprises: the mines and iron works owned by the Crown. Yet he so little understood that industrial production was becoming important socially and politically, that he proposed to found the new free Prussia exclusively upon the three preindustrial estates: a rural gentry, the professional men, merchants and artisans of the cities, and the free farmers.

It was not until the first great industrial depression, that of the 1830's, that the industrial system was recognized as a new factor. But even Marx, who scooped up and fused together the analyses and diagnoses of a great many men of that period—Conservatives and Radicals, realists and utopians—did not see that industry poses problems of social integration and political power, which are basically different from those of the mercantile society. Not only Marx's mentality, as has been often remarked, but also his society were orthodox eighteenth century and preindustrial.

Only by the end of the nineteenth century was it realized that there is a problem of industrial society. The Guild Socialists in England, Brooks and Henry Adams in the United States, Sorel in France, and the "Academic Socialists" in Germany were the first to see that the members of the industrial system are not integrated in it, and that the decisive political power in the industrial system is not legitimate power. They were the first to see that our society is not an industrial but a mercantile society, and that it can at best contain but cannot integrate the industrial reality of our times. Henry Adams' famous discovery of the dynamo as a new source of social power heralded the great crisis which reached its final and decisive stage when the United States went to war in the fall of 1941.

The clash between the organization of the mercantile society and the industrial reality shows most clearly in the two theories of economic behavior on which mercantile economic policy was based: the theory of the international division of labor which is usually known as the free-trade theory, and the theory of monopoly. Both assume a system of production under which the type and the quantity of products are more or less rigidly fixed by soil fertility, climate, and other factors beyond human control. Both, in other words, assume a preindustrial system.

Free trade is the complementary exchange of goods on the basis of a division of labor ordained by God and unchangeable by human hands. The export of British woolens against Portuguese wine was rightly the classical example of the free traders. And on that basis the expectation that free trade would bring peace was understandable. For if all trade is complementary, and if the total quantity of production is fixed, free access of all producers to all raw materials should indeed eliminate the normal causes of economic rivalry.

The theory of monopoly is equally consistent under preindustrial assumptions. If the supply is fixed within narrow limits so that it is impossible to increase it, regardless of demand, then the greatest profits are obtained through curtailment of production and maximum prices.

As soon as we substitute for the assumptions of mercantile society the realities of the industrial system, both free trade and the traditional theory of monopoly become meaningless. In the industrial system production is fixed neither in quantity nor in quality by the unchangeable conditions of nature—except within extreme limits. That today a country does not produce iron nails, and could not produce them except at a price five times as high as its neighbor, does not prove that it will not be the largest and cheapest nail producer twenty years hence. Production in the industrial system is *competitive* and not complementary. It is changing and not fixed. Free trade under these conditions becomes an attempt to freeze permanently an accidental inferiority of a country not yet fully industrialized, and to benefit permanently the country most fully industrialized at the moment. Free trade, which in the mercantile society benefited most the weakest member of the comity of nations, permanently enriches, under industrial conditions, the strongest at the expense of the weaker. It becomes not only an instrument of economic retardation but one of discrimination against new industries and new countries. This, at least, is how it appeared to the young and weak industrial system of the United States when the more advanced England of 1840 proclaimed it. And this is how it appears today to the young and weak industrial systems of the formerly raw-material-producing countries in Latin America, Asia or Africa when the United States proclaims it.

The mercantile theory of monopoly has been reduced even more to absurdity. In the industrial system there is no technological limit to production. But demand is not infinitely elastic. Hence the most profitable economic behavior is precisely the opposite from that adapted to the conditions of limited supply in a preindustrial system. Instead of a cut in production and a boost in price, maximum production and minimum price is the economically most profitable policy in an industrial system. Certainly Henry Ford made more money than all the monopolists of the old school together. He and his followers made it through monopolies or semi-monopolies which are strong because they are more efficient than small competitive enterprises could possibly be.

The old-line mercantile theory accordingly finds itself unable to attack the new monopolies. For its one argument was that monopolies must be economically inefficient. It cannot see that in the modern big business corporation it is not the question of efficiency that matters, but that of political structure and power. For the mercantile society knows no social and political problems outside of the market.

CHAPTER FOUR

THE INDUSTRIAL REALITY OF THE TWENTIETH CENTURY

THE representative social phenomena of the industrial system of our time are the mass-production plant and the corporation. The assembly line is the representative material environment; the corporation is the representative social institution. The large-scale plant has taken the place of the rural village or of the trading town of the eighteenth and early nineteenth centuries. The corporation has replaced the manor and the market as the basic institution in and through which the material reality is organized socially. And corporation management has become the decisive and representative power in the industrial system.

The corporation is usually considered an *economic* institution. But what economic function does the corporation fulfill that could not just as well be discharged by a partnership? The creation of credit requires a bank. But whether a big plant is individually or corporately owned makes no difference in its productivity, its economic efficiency or profitability. Nor does the institution of the corporation fulfill any technological function.

It is also not true that the corporation is a "conspiracy" to create privileges and monopolies, as has been so often asserted by American reformers and populists. This belief has a long history, going back to the bitter fights between the King's lawyers and the common lawyers in Tudor and early Stuart times. It was correct for the early corporation; before incorporation became accessible to everyone upon fulfillment of simple formalities, corporation and monopoly privileges were identical. The early corporation was always endowed with one of the prerogatives of the sovereign. It was to do things forbidden to all other citizens. Thus the first great corporations, the Dutch and British East India Companies, the Hudson's Bay Company or the Massachusetts Bay Company, were expressly chartered to exercise royal authority; they had their foundation in a direct delegation of sovereign power. To acquire and to rule territory overseas was at least as important a function of the first corporations as were their commercial tasks as traders or planters. In the few cases where a corporation was chartered before 1750 to do domestic business—the Bank of England is the outstanding example—it was to fulfill functions which, like the issuing of money, had been regarded from time immemorial as the inalienable monopoly rights of the sovereign. Even for another hundred years after 1750 when domestic corporations became more plentiful, they were largely confined to quasi-governmental tasks, involving an express grant of the sovereign right of eminent domain for the purpose of exploiting a "natural monopoly": turnpikes, bridges, water works, canals, railways and other "public utilities."

But although the modern corporation grew out of these chartered monopolies, it has very little in common with them except for legal forms. The modern corporation is in intent and social purpose the very opposite of the sovereign monopoly such as was the British East India Company—or such as the central banks of all countries still are. This does not mean that there are no monopolies today, or that many of them do not use the corporate form. But in the modern monopolies the corporate form is accidental, whereas it was of the essence of monopoly two hundred years ago. Before 1800 J. P. Morgan & Co. would have had to have a royal charter to obtain the position of monopoly power and privilege they had before 1907. As it is, the Morgans converted their business into a corporation precisely when they had lost most of their economic power, after 1933.

The old corporations based their authority upon the delegation of power by the political government. The new, modern corporation, the corporation which rules our industrial reality, based its authority originally upon the delegation of the individual property rights by individual citizens. It came to power as an institution of the independent social sphere of the nineteenth century, the sphere in which individual property rights gave social status and function, and generated legitimate power.

The modern corporation is thus a *political* institution; its purpose is the creation of legitimate power in the industrial sphere.

The enactment of the modern corporate laws between 1830 and 1870 was the final triumph of the mercantile society. These laws allowed any property owner to create a corporation. That a collective entity such as the corporation could be created by the free contract of individual property holders without need of any further political sanction, recognized property as an original and sovereign right. The free incorporation of the nineteenth century was the climax of the development of the bourgeois society that began with Locke's Second Treatise on Government.

The political purpose of the corporation is the creation of a legitimate social government on the basis of the original power of the individual property rights of its shareholders. The corporation is the *Contrat Social* in its purest form.

It is no coincidence that the corporation as a distinct form of organization appeared first with the theory of the social contract as formulated in the years around 1600 in North Germany and Holland, by Althusius and Grotius. And it grew to maturity in England simultaneously with the maturing of the contract theory in Locke's work. For the corporation is nothing but the contract theory transferred from the field of historical fiction or ethical justification into that of political action.

In the articles of association of a corporation founded today there is still clearly expressed the simultaneity of contract of association with contract of subjection which, according to the contract theory, creates and justifies both society and legitimate government. The limited liability of the stockholder corresponds exactly to Locke's rule that no citizen is liable for more than he has transferred to society. The free salability of the shares which enables each shareholder to resign from the association is an exact realization of the rule—expressed in its classic form by Rousseau—that each member of society must be allowed to resign by emigration. And the forms in which the stockholder-citizen exercises his "right of revolution" against the government for which he has contracted are faithful copies of the forms developed for society as a whole in Locke's Second Treatise on Government.

The purpose of the contract theory was to explain and to justify the existence of government and society as distinct from, and independent of, the existence of

the individual member. In political life the theory remained a fiction—though a powerful one. But in social
life it became reality in the corporation. In the social
contract of the corporation a social entity is actually
created through the subjection of each member's individual property rights under corporate management.
Just as the people remain sovereign in the contract theory of Locke, so the stockholders remain sovereign in
the corporation. But it is a purely normative, legal sovereignty; the sovereignty of the people as well as that
of the stockholders is the source of all legitimate power.
It institutes, limits, controls power. But it is not power
itself—a fact which many modern interpreters of the
contract theory fail to understand. Power resides in the
legitimate government—in the case of the corporation
in the duly constituted management. Management has
legitimate power because it is derived from individual
property rights. And its power remains legitimate as
long as it is based upon individual property rights.

Very few institutions in history have been as successful as the corporation. It is hardly necessary to point
out the tremendous political and social power of corporation management. Before the introduction of the
present war economy the executive of a big corporation
in any of the industrial countries had more power over
the lives and the livelihood of a greater number of people than most of the political authorities proper. The

decisions of big business management regarding prices and wages, working hours and output, shaped and molded the lives of millions of people and, ultimately, of the whole community.

But contrary to the assumptions of the contract theory, the managerial power in our industrial system is no longer based upon the property rights of the individual. It is not derived from these property rights, not controlled or limited by the holder of these rights, not responsible to them. In the modern corporation the decisive power, that of the managers, is derived from no one but from the managers themselves, controlled by nobody and nothing and responsible to no one. It is in the most literal sense unfounded, unjustified, uncontrolled and irresponsible power.

The stockholder in the modern corporation is neither willing nor able to exercise his legal sovereignty. In the great majority of cases he never casts his vote but signs a proxy made out beforehand to and by the management. He exerts no influence upon the selection of new managers who are chosen through co-option by the management in power. The stockholder exercises no influence upon the decisions of management. As a rule he neither confirms nor repudiates them; he does not even know about them and does not want to know about them. For the average stockholder today, the attraction of stock ownership over other forms of property lies precisely in the complete freedom from "bother" such as attends any other form of property ownership—the need to make or to confirm decisions, to take a part in the management or, at least, in the selection of management, the need to learn or to understand something about the business, in short the need to assume some of the responsibilities and to exercise some of the rights of ownership.

It is not true, as has often been asserted by reformers, that the stockholder has been deprived of his political rights of control and decision by a management lusting for power. The opposite is correct. The stockholder has thrust away these rights. He has abdicated, and he cannot be induced to reassume his rights. For to him they are nothing but burdens; they are entirely contrary to his purpose in becoming a stock owner.

This was shown in Germany just before Hitler came to power. For years it had been the custom of the German banks to vote in their own names the shares deposited with them by clients. The only way for a client to prevent this exercise of his right by the bank was to give explicit instructions forbidding it—a practice so rare as to be almost unknown outside of textbooks. And since the great bulk of the privately owned shares was deposited with the banks—which in Germany combined the functions of banker, stock broker, safe deposits and trust companies—the majority of the shares and with

it the decisive vote used to lie with the banks, which almost always voted with the management. During the
early years of the Depression, in the course of a reform
of the corporation law, this practice was declared illegal. In order to reinstate the stockholder into his rightful position—supposedly snatched from him by greedy
banks and dictatorial managements—it was laid down
by law that no bank could vote its depositors' shares
except upon express authorization. Contrary to the ex-
pectations of the lawmakers, the depositors—practically
without exception—gave this authorization. Many of
them even threatened the bank with withdrawal of their
clientele unless it would accept a blanket authorization
to vote all the clients' holdings at all occasions—an authorization clearly contrary to the new law for the "protection of the stockholder."

A more serious though not so blatant example is the
experience with the American Security and Exchange
Act—one of the best laws of the early New Deal. To
protect the stockholder this act requires that all corporations whose securities are listed on a stock exchange
disclose a great volume of important and relevant facts.
There is no doubt that a person with business experience
and financial understanding can learn more about the
corporation from a study of these figures and facts than
he could ever have learned before. But the normal stockholder does not want to learn anything about the poli-

cies, the decisions of the management of the corporation which is legally "his" corporation. All he knows is that the new law expects him to use a great deal of time and energy which to save is precisely the motive for his investment in shares. Not only does he not read these statements. He assumes that the fact that they are prepared according to a law and under the supervision of a government agency relieves him completely of any obligation or responsibility whatsoever. All authorities in touch with American stockholders—brokers, bankers, lawyers, investment counsels, even members of the Securities Exchange Commission—agree that the average stockholder today takes even less part in the control and management of "his" corporation than the stockholder of ten years ago.

The stockholder has not only abdicated, he has also largely become superfluous—if not in the new and weak, so in the old and successful, corporation. It is true that the record of American corporation financing, brought out in the hearings of the Temporary National Economic Committee in 1939 and 1940, covers a most unusual and atypical period: one of cheap money and simultaneous stock-exchange stagnation. Yet the extent to which one big corporation after the other succeeded in the Depression decade to finance substantial expansion programs out of internal means and without recourse to the capital market is a definite sign that the big and successful corporation can get along without the stock-holder. An investigation of German business finance from 1923 to 1933 would probably have shown the same results: financing of a tremendous expansion program through bank credits and the "plowing back" of earnings without recourse to the stock market.

The process by which ownership in the corporation has been divorced from management and control has been most publicized in the United States where Berle and Means * in their famous book more than a decade ago first portrayed it as a movement characteristic and typical of modern industrialism. Subsequent studies, especially one by Marshal E. Dimock,** have shown that the development has been gathering momentum during the depression years. American political and economic thinking alone has understood the full implications of the process. But American actual developments—up to America's formal entry into the war—had seemingly not progressed as far in the direction of the divorce of ownership and control as had developments in prewar England and pre-Hitler Germany.

In the United States the decisive power at least still rested with the management of the corporation proper. But in prewar England and in pre-Hitler Germany the decisive power in the industrial system had largely

---

* Berle and Means: *The Modern Corporation and Private Property*.
** In No. 11 of the T.N.E.C. monographs.

passed to a management outside of the corporation: to the managers of cartels, industrial federations, *Spitzenverbaende*, etc. The executive secretaries or directors of these managers' associations largely determined prices, labor policies, and wages. In the most powerful associations—such as the British Iron and Steel Federation, the International Steel Cartel or the German Cement Cartel —they also determined output and margin of profit. While these association managers themselves were responsible to and controlled by the managers of the member firms of the association, they were completely beyond reach of stockholders' control. The distribution of the cement quota among the member firms of the German Portland Cement Cartel or the distribution of the tin-plate quota among the members of the British Iron and Steel Federation determined not only output and profits, but often the survival or disappearance of the business. Yet the cartel managers' power was founded on nothing but the absolute and uncontrolled managerial will.

But it was in the United States and not in Europe where managerial power was officially enthroned as autonomous and uncontrolled power. The National Recovery Act (NRA) Codes of 1933 and 1934 not only provided for compulsory cartels in all industries; they also left the stockholder without legal rights. These Codes were declared unconstitutional by the Supreme

Court and the previous legal system was restored. But industrial reality never went back. During the thirties it always conformed more closely to the NRA pattern than to the assumptions of nineteenth-century corporation laws or to economic rules.

The difference between Europe and America is not a difference in political development. The only reason why there are no cartels in the United States is that they are illegal under the antitrust laws. But while the antitrust laws prevented the cartelization of American industry, they undoubtedly furthered the growth of the mammoth corporations in which management is as independent of stockholder control as is the executive of a cartel. In Europe two or three competing firms would come to an agreement as separate companies about prices, wages, and sales quota. But merger was the only way to reach the same end in the United States. For while agreement in restraint of trade is illegal, merger is not. Every student of American business history knows numerous examples—old and recent—in which actual corporate merger was the form chosen to realize marketing or price agreements. The antitrust laws which were enacted in order to protect the small fellow thus led in many cases to his actual extinction, since they made impossible noncompetitive survival as a member of a cartel.

Both in the American mammoth corporation and in the European trade federation or *Spitzenverband* the stockholder has no decision or responsibility. And in both he wants none. In neither is managerial power actually derived from, or traceable to, stock ownership; that is, to individual property rights. The decisive political authority in the industrial system, the modern corporate management—whether nominally a servant of the stockholders as in America, or legally completely unconnected with the stockholders like the management of cartels and *Spitzenverbaende*—is not the executive agent of the atoms of individual property joined together socially in the corporation. It is not power delegated by property. Management power has become original power.

Actually, this is still an understatement. It is not only true that management in the modern corporate system is independent of and uncontrolled by the holders of individual property rights. It is equally true that ownership of stock in the modern corporation is no longer property in the corporation in any but the most formal sense. All it represents is a vested and legally protected right to a participation in future profits in consideration of past services. Nobody buys a share today except as a share in earnings—or in order to benefit from an increase in the price of the stock which will follow from the expectation of higher earnings. In other words, the present-day investor does not want a property right. He wants a share in whatever profits result from somebody else's exercise of property rights; and that somebody else is the management. Actually, the stockholder regards the management as the real sovereign in the corporation, holding original power as if it owned the corporation. He sees himself only as the beneficiary of an extremely limited right of usufruct.

That in the last analysis there is no ownership in the assets of the corporation has already found expression in the legal and institutional treatment of the corporation. The most radical legal expression of the change is the Nazi corporation law which treats the corporation as an organic autonomous social entity in which management has direct, indigenous and sovereign power under the "leader principle." The stockholder has no rights. He receives the dividend allotted to him by the government or by the management; but he has no vote, especially no vote against the management. This new legal concept of the corporation consciously repudiates the contract theory from which the corporation had originally been developed—an inevitable repudiation from the Nazi point of view, of course. It also repudiates the claim of property to be the legitimate basis of social power—again a logical step for Nazism. It proclaims that corporate property is different in kind from individual property, and that ownership of individual property can give no property rights over corporate property. In other words, it proclaims that corporate property is not property in the traditional sense but something new and basically different.

The Nazi corporation law is the most complete break with the traditional legal and political concept of property. Even Soviet Russia did not go so far. Actually, the Bolsheviks kept the traditional property concept in all its Lockean purity. It is, after all, the essence of Marxism that it accepts property ownership as the legitimate basis of political and social power. Only on the basis of the politically constitutive character of property ownership can the Marxist justify his demand that all property should be owned by the sovereign people as the rightful fountainhead of all power.

Yet, although the Nazi corporation law sweepingly renounces and repeals all traditional political assumptions and beliefs regarding the nature and meaning of property, the German stockholders did not seem to think that anything had happened. There have been no reports of stock sales on account of the new laws. The German shareholder obviously felt that the new laws only codified what had been actual social reality for a long time before.

The United States has not yet enacted any drastic change in its corporation laws. Yet as experienced a man as Owen D. Young—perhaps the best representative of modern professional corporate management—proposed over ten years ago to deprive the stockholder of his legal property title, to vest property rights in the management, and to pay the stockholder a "wage" for the use of his money. Such a legal concept of the corporation would conform far more accurately to reality than do our present laws which describe the corporation of a hundred years ago. For many years the American shareholder has been used to shares without voting power—shares expressing a mere right of usufruct without carrying the political rights of property ownership. And the bankruptcy law enacted during the Depression—a law which the stockholder generally regards as favorable to him—expressly treats corporate property and corporate management as autonomous, and the stockholder's property as a mere claim to future profits.

However, the most radical change in the status of the stockholder has come in this war, not through legal reforms but through the war system of taxation. Both in the United States and in England it is now the government which occupies the former position of the common-share holder and which has the direct stake in profits and losses. Under the wartime excess profits taxes of both countries the common-share holder's return is "frozen." An increase in profits goes entirely to the government. And due to the high level of corporation taxes, the government is also the chief loser if there is a decrease—

although the shareholder, too, participates to a minor extent in a reduction of income. Altogether the common shares have become—at least for the duration—very precariously secured preferred shares. The equity position formerly occupied by the common shares has almost entirely been assumed by the Treasury.

A good example is the case of one of the largest American retail companies which in the last peace-year sold almost $1,000,000,000 of goods, and which cleared a profit of approximately seven dollars per share. Under the wartime excess profits tax the stockholder cannot receive more than $3.50 in dividends which corresponds to the average earnings on a $500,000,000 turnover. The company could thus lose half its business before the stockholder's share would be affected. On the other hand, his return cannot increase no matter how prosperous the company. All possible increases in earnings benefit only the Treasury, and the Treasury is also the only loser as long as profits do not fall below fifty per cent of the last peace-year. The common-share holder is thus indeed confined to the "wage" for his capital which Owen D. Young proposed.

Both in the United States and in Germany there have been corporations which were actually owned by no one —not even legally. There were, before the Depression, the potash companies in Germany which were under the same management and owned each other without outside

shareholders at all. In the United States some of the
"pyramided holding companies" particularly in the In-
sull utilities empire, achieved the same end by a com-
bination of "voting trusts," intercompany holdings of
shares and intercompany financing. Yet, although there
was no owner, these corporations functioned as such and
were managed by "duly elected" directors who in turn
"appointed" the executive officers; and they undoubtedly
had tremendous properties. Could anyone have said who
owned these properties? Or was it not true that these
corporations owned themselves? And what remained of
the assumptions on which had been based the eighteenth-
and nineteenth-century theory of property and of the
institution of the corporation: that all property must be
owned by someone, and that the social and political
power in the corporation derives its legitimacy from individual property rights?

The corporation has become an autonomous social entity—in no way different today from, for instance, a city
or any other political entity. There can be no rights of
property in an autonomous organic social entity since it
must be conceived of as existing independent of, and
before, the members. There can only be rights against
such an entity: claims; and rights within it: governmental authority. The stockholder today actually only
owns a claim; the management exercises authority. But

on what basis does this authority rest if there is no longer the basis of individual property rights?

The abdication of individual property rights as a basis of social power is the central institutional change of our times. It has already had tremendous consequences.

In the first place, the development of the corporation to an autonomous social entity which exercises power by its own authority, has made meaningless the discussion between capitalism and socialism—at least in the terms and with the assumptions that have been traditionally used. Both orthodox capitalism and orthodox socialism assume not only that property is a legitimate basis of power, but also that property *is* social power. Neither can admit the possibility of a divorce under which social power would become independent of property, and property would become socially powerless. Both the orthodox capitalist and the orthodox Marxist start with the axiom that property is socially constitutive. They differ only on who should own. But they agree that the ownership of property must decide the nature and structure of society and of social power—precisely because they agree on the nature and political meaning of property. In their discussions of property, Locke, Adam Smith and Hamilton are a good deal more "Marxist" than Marx.

But ownership today is not socially constitutive. The form in which property is owned does no longer decide who wields the power. We have seen this quite clearly in the two revolutions of our times. The Communist nationalization of private property did not result in the equality that would have followed had the capitalist-socialist assumptions been true. The concentration of power in government hands and the totalitarianism of the régime had nothing to do with the nationalization of property. The Soviet system is based on the transfer of total control to the government which could just as well—if not better—have been effected without any change in the legal title of ownership.

This has been proved by the second revolution of our times—that of the Nazis. They have made no legal changes in the property sphere. Yet they have abolished private initiative, private social power and the "free enterprise" system as effectively as have the Communists. Nobody at all familiar with the Nazi system would maintain that it is "capitalism" in any political sense of the word. Yet it maintained private property and profits as legal fictions—simply because these institutions do not matter politically in the industrial system. They were easier to maintain than to destroy, especially as their destruction would not have increased the efficiency of the total control of the party-state.

Since the war started, every belligerent country has learned the lesson the Nazis have taught: property does not matter politically. All that matters is control, which today is divorced from and independent of property rights. Total political control is the essence of modern war economics. And while it makes property rights politically meaningless and nonexistent, it does not and need not change or eliminate property.

For the future this means that the basic political issues will center on control and not, as in the past, on property. We can see that clearly in contemporary economic and political thinking. We no longer talk about the "private property system" but about "free enterprise" and "private initiative."

The only consistent and effective contemporary theory of capitalism—that of Professor Joseph Schumpeter—neither attempts to justify property nor tries to see property as constitutive in the social structure or as the motive power of economic development. Schumpeter centers on private initiative; the enterprising manager is both the justification and the motive power of this capitalist system. Capital plays a most subordinate part. Without the enterprising manager, Schumpeter regards it as wholly unproductive; it is nothing but an auxiliary to management. Professor Schumpeter is hard pressed to find a convincing justification for capital's claim to a share in the profits. One gathers that he would consider compensation beyond a service fee as an unjustified increment, and as a "surplus value" which properly should have gone to management.

On the other hand, the socialists too have been shift-ing their emphasis from property to control. The "ex-propriation of all means of production" is something very different from "social planning," which has become the essence of modern collectivist thought. Planning is simply another name for control; and that it is seen as the essence of a new socialist society is a confession that control, not property rights, matters. Even where the old slogans cannot be given up and where nationalization is still regarded as an important aim, it is the nationaliza-tion of controls that is aimed at. Thus the British Labour Party's demand for a "nationalisation of the banks" which became official party policy during the thirties—formerly it had always been nationalization of railways or steel mills—was a demand for the nationalization of a control. Banks do not produce goods but control their production or distribution.*

This does not mean that private property will disap-pear in the society of the future. On the contrary, indi-vidual property should be maintained; and attacks on it might cease. Just as religious freedom became a uni-

---

* The Labour Party platform was based upon a thorough misunder-standing of the nature of credit. And it failed to see that commercial banks today are "nationalised" anyhow as their policies are completely controlled by Treasury and Central Bank policies or requests. Yet, while meaningless in practice, this switch of the Labour Party from national-ization of property to nationalization of controls grew out of a correct, though probably subconscious, appraisal of the actual social develop-ment.

versally recognized and granted right as soon as religion
ceased to be constitutive of Western society, so individual property should become universally recognized
and generally granted if it no longer carries political
power or control. If it is understood that to own a house
has as little political meaning as whether one is a Baptist
or a Presbyterian, then there will be no objection at all
against individual property. Governments would be able
to promote the individual ownership of personal property as a matter of course.

This brings us to the final and most important conclusion from our analysis: Managerial power today is
illegitimate power. It is in no way based upon a fundamental principle accepted by society as a legitimate
basis of power. It is not controlled by such a principle
nor limited by it. And it is responsible to no one. Individual property was a fundamental principle accepted
by society as a legitimate basis of social and political
power. The limitations, controls, and responsibilities of
management were those set or imposed by the individual
shareholders exercising jointly and severally their individual property rights. Western society is still willing
to accept individual property rights as a good title to
legitimate power. But today managerial power is independent of, uncontrolled by, and not responsible to the
shareholders. And there is no other fundamental prin-

ciple to take the place of individual property rights as a legitimate basis for the power which management actually wields.

Altogether, our industrial economy has become split into two parts: a "real" economy of plants, mills, machines, managers and workers, and a "symbol" economy of negotiable securities, legal titles and empty ownership rights. The "real" economy is organized in "going concerns"—the significantly vague term American jurisprudence has coined for something that really does not fit into the legal system of property rights. The "going concern" is taken to exist outside and beyond the property rights of the shareholders and to be unaffected by the fluctuations and fortunes of the market. Everywhere we find economic policy today based on the assumption that the "going concern" must be maintained and strengthened, even at the price of jettisoning both stockholders and the price system of the market. The "symbol" economy, on the other hand, is of the market. In it are observed the nineteenth-century assumptions regarding the position of property.

But only in the "real" economy is there social power and control. The "symbol" economy gives wealth; but wealth by itself no longer confers social power. The rulers in the "real" economy might have to be content with a good income and they might never accumulate large fortunes. But they, and they alone, have power.

Yet their power rests in no way upon the symbols of property rights and ownership. Only in legal fiction is the "real" economy still dependent upon, and directed by, the symbols. Actually, the "symbol" economy has become a powerless appendix to the "real" economy—if there is any connection at all.

Lest I be misunderstood: this is *not* an attack upon modern management. On the contrary, there has never been a more efficient, a more honest, a more capable and conscientious group of rulers than the professional management of the great American corporations today. The power they wield is theirs not because they usurped it, but because the stockholder has relinquished his rights and his duties. Most of the corporation executives I know are unhappy in their positions of uncontrolled and nonresponsible social power which they did not seek, but into which they have been pushed.

A clear indication of their acute discomfort can be seen in their attempts to develop a legitimate basis for their power in "service." The campaign to have the services rendered by management to the community, rather than the property rights of the stockholders, accepted as a basis of managerial rule was by no means all hypocrisy or supersalesmanship. Most of the managers took it seriously.

However, honesty, efficiency and capability have never been and never will be good titles to power. The questions whether power is legitimate or illegitimate, whether a ruler is a constitutional ruler or a despot lie altogether on a plane different from that of personal qualities. Bad qualities can vitiate a good title. But good personal qualities can never remedy the lack of title. Nor is the despot against his will any less a despot. All that is likely to result from his attempts to shirk the power that has been thrust upon him, is timidity and insecurity which only aggravate the situation. A good man on a usurper's throne will probably rule for a shorter time than the bandit who does not care about the title as long as he has the power; at least the bandit will act and will fight for his power.

It was this insight which earned Machiavelli most of the opprobrium which has been heaped upon him. At a time when there was no legitimate rule and no legitimate basis for power—at least not in his native Italy— he saw that the bandit was more likely to succeed and to prevail than the honest, scrupulous, conscientious prince. And although his conclusion is most unpalatable to all honest men, it is a correct one. The answer to Machiavelli is not honest and enlightened despots, but legitimate rulers. The answer to the illegitimacy of present-day managerial rule is not to "turn the rascals out"—there are not many anyhow—but to make the ruling power in the industrial system a legitimate power.

Unless and until this is done, the industrial system will have no legitimate power.

2.

If the corporation is the representative social institution and if management is the decisive social power, mass production in big units is the representative social form of our society. The big centralized concentrated mass-production unit may not be quantitatively in the majority—neither in the number of workers employed nor in the volume of output. Yet the attempt to use these quantitative measurements for the qualitative purpose of proving that ours is actually still a "small unit" technology is ridiculous in the extreme. It does not matter what the statistical averages are. The big mass-producing unit may statistically be an isolated case, as in England before 1939. It may be less efficient technically than the small or medium-sized factory. The big automatic mechanized plant may even be economically unprofitable. But mechanized mass production in big units is the technological form of industrial production which matters most, politically and socially.

Mass production is the "ideal type" of modern industrial production which directly or indirectly molds all our concepts, methods and aims of industrial production altogether. It would be but slight exaggeration to say that our whole industrial society changed basically on the day, thirty-five years ago, when Henry Ford first used the assembly-line method consciously as a radically new system of production. Certainly since then no industrial country has ever been the same, even in Europe where the assembly line itself was very slow in gaining ground.

The new mass-production system carries all the technological and economic momentum; it is the dynamic force in our techno-economic engine.

If we analyze this representative system of industrial production, we shall find that its new basic feature is not a new use of, or approach to, machinery. There is no difference in the treatment of the inanimate tools of production. When we call the new system "automatic" or "mechanized," we do not mean that the machines have become automatic or mechanical. What has become automatic and mechanical is the worker.

The great innovation of modern industry is a vision: a vision of the worker as an efficient, automatic, standardized machine. Whether the credit for this vision should go to Henry Ford, to Taylor, or to the behaviorist psychologists is a moot point. Like all great discoveries, it was probably made at the same time by different people working and thinking independently. Around 1900, the whole emphasis of industry changed. Up till then, for a hundred and fifty years, the most skilled, the most highly trained worker was the most efficient, the most productive, the most valuable worker. Suddenly, the very qualities which made the good craftsman —understanding of the process, knowledge of all its phases, initiative, the personal touch, etc.—became obstacles to efficiency and productivity. Uniformity, absence of any personal relationship to the work, specialization on one unskilled manipulation, subdivision of the work into particles without comprehensible cohesion became the new way to maximum productivity and efficiency.

It may be said that the era before mass production was just as much based upon the unskilled, mechanized laborer as our present productive system. All the descriptions of the mills in Manchester, Liverpool or Glasgow in the early stages of the Industrial Revolution emphasize the almost dehumanized hordes of starved, illiterate, dispossessed semi-savages from Ireland and Scotland who slaved on the early power spindles and power looms. But this was not efficient labor—no more so than are today the illiterate, unskilled labor in Malayan rubber plantations, or the Negroes in the cotton fields of the American South. The unskilled workers of the early industrial stage were so inefficient that they could be used economically only at starvation wages. They were employed only because skilled, self-respecting workers could not be obtained.

Most manufacturers in the century before 1914 or 1929 firmly believed that a more highly skilled, more individualist worker would be a better worker. They were forever starting trade schools or endowing poly-technical institutes. Actually, all during the nineteenth century there was a definite trend away from the un-skilled, automatic worker to the craftsman. If there ever should be a statistical investigation of the develop-ment of labor skills during the nineteenth century, it will certainly show that at the close of the century the proportion of unskilled, automatic workers was much lower than it had been at the beginning.

Today, however, the automatic mechanized worker is the most efficient worker, producing the most per unit of labor. There is not only a rapid trend toward the complete mechanization of all but a few workers which has been greatly accelerated by the Depression and by the present war. There is also a prestige attached to it; to go automatic is to be progressive. The most con-vincing examples of the change are in the old industries —the same industries which started a hundred and fifty years ago with human automata but had managed to develop their own craftsmen in the meantime. As old, as efficient and as specialized an industry as the New York garment industry has, since the Depression, suf-fered greatly from the competition of a new, fully mechanized, automatic clothing industry in St. Louis and Kansas City. The fact that women's wear seems least amenable to standardization, in view of the rapid fashion changes in the United States, apparently proved no obstacle to the assembly-line process.

It is sometimes argued that the mechanization and automatization of the worker in modern mass-production industry is but a transitory stage to the complete elimination of manual labor. An automatic steel strip mill or an automatic plate-glass plant operate seemingly without manual labor at all. A handful of highly skilled operators on control boards—junior executives rather than workers—do the work formerly performed by hundreds or thousands of skilled manual workers. What has happened is not that the former manual laborers have now become skilled control-board operators. Today, only the former foremen are left while the former laborers have disappeared. Whether they have become the victims of technological unemployment, or whether they are now human automata serving machines producing far more than they ever could have produced in the old way, is immaterial for our point. Even the assumption of the "technocrats" of 1933 memory does not invalidate our argument. For if it should really be true that a consistent application of modern mass-production methods would produce a superabundance of goods, practically without any labor, then the former industrial worker would no longer have status and function in the productive process. And a society like ours, which sees social status and function predominantly in status and function in the economic process, could not integrate the functionless industrial worker—even though it might be able to supply him abundantly with goods.

That the employed wórker in modern mass-production industry has no social status and function is usually overlooked by modern writers who have been taught that nothing counts in social life except income and economic wealth. But even they have noticed the social and political problem of the *unemployed* worker in modern society.

The mass unemployment of the "long armistice" was an entirely new phenomenon. In no previous depression was there any chronic unemployment. Indeed, if we accept the results of recent research, there was no unemployment at all in the most severe business crisis of the nineteenth century, that of 1873. But even when there was unemployment it was the last of the crisis phenomena to come, and the first to go. In the past, unemployment had always disappeared long before the recovery showed in higher stock and commodity prices or in bigger industrial profits. In the last Depression, however, the unemployment problem improved last—if it improved at all.

Actually, the most frightening thing about the industrial unemployment of the last twenty years was that it persisted through periods of recovery, and, indeed, of high prosperity. There remained an irreducible core of unemployment in the Germany of 1927, the England of 1935, the United States of 1937—all years of record or near-record industrial activity. This is not just a sign of economic dislocation. It is a most serious symptom of social disruption. For unemployment is not only an economic catastrophe. It is a social disfranchisement. The unemployed has lost his livelihood as well as his status and function in society. He is an outcast—for a man who has no function and no status, for whom society has no use and nothing to do, has been cast out.

We all know that unemployment cannot be cured by economic relief. In countries where the "dole" was almost as high as the wages of unskilled labor, the social effects of unemployment showed almost as fully as in countries where there was no organized relief at all. Above all, the unemployed disintegrated socially. He lost his skills, he lost his morale, he became apathetic and asocial. The unemployed may be bitter at first; resentment is still a form of participation in society, if only in protest. But soon society becomes too irrational, too incomprehensible to the unemployed even for rebellion. He becomes bewildered, frightened, resigned, and sinks finally into an apathy which is almost a living social death.

During the twilight periods of high business activity with high unemployment which characterized the industrial countries during the recent past, any social worker with experience could point out the chronically unemployed from among the Saturday evening crowd in an industrial town. They were not necessarily dressed more shabbily than the others; they did not look any more underfed than many of the employed workers in the crowd. But they had an unmistakable air of bewilderment, of defeat and blind purposelessness that set them apart fully as much as if they had belonged to another race. And in a sense they did. Around them had grown an invisible wall separating them from the members of a society which had cast them out. Not only the unemployed but society too felt this wall. Social intercourse between employed and unemployed ceased gradually. They frequented different taverns and different poolrooms, hardly intermarried and generally kept to themselves. There are no more tragic and no more frightening pages in the whole literature of chronic unemployment than those which tell of the destruction through unemployment of man's most basic community: the family. Many a fully unemployed family maintained its social unity, its social cohesion and its social strength—but hardly any partly unemployed family survived as a functioning community. Unemployed father and employed children, unemployed children and employed father, unemployed brother and employed sister—became separated by a wall of mutual suspicion and mutual incomprehensibility, which neither love nor necessity could breech.

If there is any further proof needed for the social meaning of unemployment, it is provided by the gambling of the unemployed in all industrial countries. The popularity of football pools and dog races in England or of the "numbers game" in the United States cannot be explained by the desire of the unemployed to make a few pennies the only way they could. The unemployed knew that they were bound to lose as well as any sermonizing editorial writer calculating the odds. But blind, unreasoning chance appeared to the unemployed the only operative force in this world and in this society; only chance made sense. And football pools or numbers games were seemingly the only rational conduct in a society without other rationality, without meaning, sense, function and integrating power.

It is absolutely certain that we shall have to prevent a recurrence of large-scale chronic unemployment after this war. Otherwise, we shall surely disintegrate into chaos or tyranny. But it is not enough to find productive work for the unemployed, though it is the first thing to do.

However, this would only solve the problem of economic security and not that of social function and status, which is a problem of the employed worker as well as of the unemployed. The social problem of the industrial worker in the modern industrial system may be likened to an iceberg. Unemployment is the part that shows above the water. But the real bulk, the real danger, lies below waterline. It is the increasing lack of function and status of the employed worker. We may get rid of the obvious danger: the unemployment. But unless we also attack the much greater, though less obvious, problem of the social function of the employed worker, we will founder.

We do not have to examine the consequences of automatic mass production to arrive at the conclusion that the worker in modern industry lacks social status and function as an individual. Denial of the existence of an individual with social status and function is really the essence of the new approach. In mass production technology the worker is only one sloppily designed machine. To bring this human machine to the full mechanical and automatic efficiency which its Maker apparently failed to achieve is the main aim of the new science of "human engineering." That means, however, that the individual must cease to exist. The new technique demands standardized, freely interchangeable, atomic labor without status, without function, without individuality. It demands graded tools. But there is no relationship between the worker's function as part of a precision machine which the present-day industrial system assigns to him, and any individual purpose. From the point of view of the system the individual worker functions only, makes sense only, is rational only when he ceases to be a member of society. From the point of view of the individual worker the society of the mass-production age does not and cannot make sense at all.

Certainly the unskilled laborer did not hold such an enviable position in the productive system of yesterday. The wheelbarrow pusher in a steel plant, the sewing-machine operator in a garment sweatshop, the Irish navvies in a railroad construction gang, had a hard life indeed, much harder than the mechanized assembly-line worker of today. But the unskilled worker of the last generation was an inferior. Often he was a recent immigrant from central or southern Europe (in the United States), from Ireland or Russia (in England), from Bohemia or Poland (in Germany and France). He did not speak the language and he came from countries that were considered "backward." Or the unskilled worker of yesterday was the individual failure, the "shiftless and thriftless," of the early capitalist society. That those workers were not integrated into society could be rationally explained.

Above all, the unskilled worker of the nineteenth century was an auxiliary. He was necessary to help the real workers; but none of the skilled people would have called him a worker. He brought materials to the skilled people. He carted off their semifinished or finished products, or he performed a type of labor which, like digging the soil, was basically preindustrial in technique. The real worker was a craftsman with all the craftsman's pride, understanding, skill and status. No one could be prouder, more self-respecting and more firmly aware of his relationship to society than an old-line printer, railroad engineer or machinist.

But in the new system the unskilled mechanized worker is the real worker. The skilled craftsmen have become the auxiliaries who prepare and lay out the job but who do not do it themselves. The productive labor is that of the man on the assembly line who, standing rigidly all day, holds in his outstretched hand a paint brush which automatically draws a red line on the flanks of slowly passing automobile bodies. He neither understands how an automobile works nor does he possess any skill which could not be acquired by everyone within a few days. He is not a human being in society, but a freely replaceable cog in an inhumanly efficient machine.

3.

That the industrial system neither provides social status and function for the individual nor establishes a legitimate social power is not a very new discovery. Especially in the last ten years there has appeared a vast amount of "crisis literature" dealing with the social problems of our time. And there have been a considerable number of proposals how to solve these problems. Some of them merit a short discussion, if only because they have been widely acclaimed as panaceae. Actually, all of them are at best palliatives. They might mitigate some of the symptoms but they do not attack the causes. By and large, they are not solutions for the future but unfinished business of the past.

Economic security is the most popular cure-all. I want to say at the outset that a considerable measure of economic security will be a "must" in the industrial countries after the Western democracies have won the war. We know that in peacetime we can produce enough of all essentials of life for everybody. The war has added the realization that production can always be made to run at full capacity with the aid of direct governmental intervention into production and investment. The new techniques of distribution—rationing, communal feeding, distribution of essentials outside the market (such as that most promising of all beginnings, the Food Stamp Plan in the United States)—have shown that it is possible to distribute existing supplies equitably. It is most unlikely that the people in any belligerent country after this war will allow large numbers to go without essentials in times of potential or actual surplus when there has been a reasonably equitable distribution in times of shortage. As far as economic security means "security from want" and a guarantee of the basic necessities of life, we can assume that it will be a fact after this war in any country capable of producing the basic necessities in abundance. This means, of course, the United States in the first place.

Actually, we had a very substantial measure of economic security in the Western world before the outbreak of the war. The panicky fear of insecurity which was characteristic of the years before the war arose at a time which offered more economic security than any previous period. Never before in Western history had there been such ample economic provision for the needy and the unemployed as in the Depression years with their doles, relief payments, WPA's, etc. It sounds strange, but it is a fact, that as a result of the relief program actual nutritional conditions in the United States were better in 1935 or 1938 than they had been in 1928 or 1929.

This shows that economic security in itself is not the solution. What the people really demanded during the last decade was not only economic security, but social status and function. Not knowing what it was they lacked, they called for economic remedies; after all, they had been taught for almost two hundred years that economic measures and rewards alone matter. Yet one need only look at the case histories of relief recipients or of workers on the WPA to see that what they needed and lacked was the social integration, the social function and status which economic security could never have given by itself and never did give.

Minimum economic security—the guarantee of an adequate supply of the basic essentials for all—will be an accomplished fact in the democracies of the West. This will be true even before the end of the war—if the war lasts more than another year or two. It may not be called "economic security" but may go by some technical name such as "purchasing-power rationing," under which it is at present being advocated in the United States and in England. Whatever it is called, the essence will be the same: the equal distribution of basic necessities regardless of individual income. That part of the program which limits the purchases of essentials by the well-to-do should indeed disappear after the war. But that part which subsidizes the poor to enable them to obtain an adequate minimum supply will certainly remain once it has been introduced.

Economic security necessitates a far greater degree of paternalism than anything ever tried under a free society. The fears and objections of those who see in the demand for it a program for tyranny cannot simply be dismissed as "reactionary." And the argument of the supporters of economic security that free public schools or highways were also once decried as "socialism" is not a very strong one. The concentration of economic power necessary for a program of economic security will be compatible with a free government only if there are carefully prepared limitations, new institutional vehicles of self-government, and a rigid decentralization. But it is not impossible to set up institutions that will safeguard society against the political danger of economic security. Undoubtedly there also will be people who will abuse what is conceived as a protection against undeserved and unnecessary want. But, on the whole, the danger that economic security will demoralize vast masses seems greatly exaggerated. Altogether the gulf between the guaranteed minimum security and the standard of consumption which is regarded even today as a moderate standard in the United States should be so great as to eliminate the danger of a large-scale lapse into government-backed loafing. But even if economic security is completely divested of the last traces of paternal despotism, it will still not be a constructive basis of a functioning society. It will not give social status and function to the individual member of society.

Economic security as a political program ignores the most important lesson of the last twenty-five years: that economic satisfactions are only negatively effective in society and politics. The absence of economic satisfactions creates severe social and political dislocations. But their presence does not by itself constitute a functioning society. Economic satisfactions can be likened to vitamins; their absence creates deficiency diseases of a most serious nature, but they do not in themselves provide calories.

It is the great strength of agrarianism and unionism that they see the organization of society as the central problem of our time. Indeed, both talk not just about social organization but about a way of life—about basic beliefs, about the social order, about man's nature and its fulfillment. Both contain much that I hope will be realized in the industrial society of the future. There is the agrarian's insistence upon the vital place of individual property in society—not as a basis of political or social power, not as control over the means of production, but as purely personal property, as a basis for human dignity and independence. There is the unionist's demand that labor be treated not as a commodity but as a partner with a right to self-government and to human dignity. And both philosophies realize that we are living in a great social crisis today—a crisis which centers on the order of the industrial system. Yet while both contain much that is promising, important and constructive, neither seems equipped to provide a solution and to build a functioning industrial society. If and when we have developed such a solution, we shall probably look back upon these two philosophies as fore-runners—but as nothing more than that.

All agrarian movements or philosophies—whether they talk of the "co-operative way of life," of small family farms, or of garden cities—start out by repudiating the industrial reality. They all talk of building a functioning society. But they begin by shirking the issue: our society does not function precisely because it is not an industrial but a preindustrial, mercantile and rural one.

This is clearly realized by those who advocate unionism as the "realistic," as the typically industrial solution. It is unionism that is usually meant when people talk about "industrial democracy."

However "realistic" the industrial democracy of unionism might appear at first sight, it is the greatest mirage of our times. It is certain to end not in a free but in a despotic society. It also could never bring about a functioning society where the individual would be socially integrated, and where social and political power would be legitimate. Agrarianism, while a romantic escape, has at least a noble vision of a society built on the independence, responsibility and dignity of man. But unionism as a social creed is a misunderstanding.

In our present political and social system, trade-unions are beneficial and necessary. The worker needs the organization and protection which only the unions can give. Trade-unions as the organization of labor, are the necessary, almost inevitable concomitant to the managerial and big-business structure of modern industry. In our existing system of industrial organization, they are also an extremely efficient method of labor-management—so much so that a strong, independent and honest union is as much of an asset for management as for the workers.

The trade-union is beneficial and desirable today because it counterbalances some of the more obvious ills of our social body. It is an anti-organization, an antibody against social toxins. But it is not a constructive institution—nor designed as one. It is only possible and only meaningful as the counterweight to the big-business management in our present society. But it is just as little controlled, responsible or legitimate power. Unionism is basically a corrective and, as such, extremely valuable. It is a brace needed by a social body suffering from curvature of the spine. It cannot create a healthy body or do anything but damage if used on one.

The greatest illusion of the advocates of unionism as a social philosophy or a political program is their belief that the power in the trade-union is legitimate power. Their argument is simply that trade-union leaders are elected by the majority vote of the members and hence are both democratic and legitimate. The same people would angrily denounce the argument that modern corporation management is elected by the majority of the stockholders and hence both democratic and legitimate. They would point out that election and control of corporate management by the stockholders are a legal sham, and that in reality management is self-appointed, uncontrolled and almost completely removed from the individual property rights of the stockholders. But precisely the same is true of modern union leadership—and for the same reasons. The individual union member is like the individual stockholder; he neither wants to exercise his individual rights, nor would he know how to do it and for what purpose. Just as the stockholder buys a share in a modern big-business corporation because he thereby escapes the decisions and responsibilities of ownership, so the individual union member joins the union in order to escape decisions and to transfer the burden of responsibility to the union leader.

The one occasion when the union member exercises his membership right to choose his leadership is, as in the case of the corporation stockholder, after a catastrophe. A lost strike may lead to the ejection of the union leaders, just as a succession of bad years or bankruptcy may lead to the removal of the corporation management by the stockholders. But in each case a new management is promptly put in to be as uncontrolled and uncontrollable as the old one was. Actually, the modern union is a good deal less democratic than the corporation, as far as its internal organization goes. The stockholder can always sell his shares, whereas the union member must remain a member on pain of losing his livelihood. So far as society is concerned, there is no difference between the corporation management's claim to political and social power and the union leader's demand for such power. Neither has a real and legitimate basis; the majority decision of the union membership is as much a fiction as the majority decision of the stockholder's individual property rights. This is as true for unions which strictly observe all rules, hold elections, publish reports and try to educate their members to participate actively in union affairs, as for those unions—not unknown in the United States—which have not held an election in ten years, are ruled by strong-arm methods and do not permit their members any expression of opinion other than regular payment of dues. For it is the union membership which does not want the power and responsibility which is fictionally theirs. If there is any union in which the members actively elect and direct their leaders, it is only the weak and struggling one—just as the shareholders usually take an active part in the management of a young corporation in its development stage. As soon as a union or a corporation is strong and well established, management of necessity becomes self-perpetuating and absolute.

Modern union leadership is simply the counterpart of modern corporation management. It has been developed to deal with corporation management, and it operates on the same principles. It is the negative to the corporation's positive. The difference between them is so small that it might pass unnoticed if the union leaders were to change places with the industrial managers. In every industrial country business management and union leadership follow the same pattern of personalities and policies. There is a striking similarity between the qualities that in England make for success in the trade associations, cartels, and industrial federations—the seat of the actual managerial power in that country—and the qualities that characterize the successful British trade-union secretary. But for the fact that they went to different schools, the two are interchangeable. Yet this type of the "functionary" is otherwise rather rare in English public life. The same was true in pre-Hitler Germany: The conscientious, pedantic, legalistic and unimaginative trade-union bureaucrat and the equally conscientious and unimaginative cartel or trade-association bureaucrat, Syndikus, Chamber of Commerce Secretary, etc., were of one piece.

The most striking confirmation of this thesis can be seen in the United States. The trade-union leaders of the last generation, a Samuel Gompers or a William Green, faithfully mirrored the conservative and rather timid banker or corporation-counsel management of the years before the War of 1914. The leadership of the new trade-unions which sprang up during the Depression resembled nothing more than the public utility tycoons of pyramided holding companies and the jerrybuilders of spectacular but purely speculative industrial empires who dominated the American industrial scene in the twenties. And already—following the trend in corporation management with only a few years' lag—a new type of union leader is coming up: the career man and efficiency expert who think in terms of the union as an autonomous institutional entity, just as modern management thinks of the corporation.

To substitute union leadership for corporation management as the foremost if not as the decisive power as the union creed demands would not make for any real change in the structure of society. The rulers would be changed, but not the rule. Such a change would not establish the first prerequisite of a functioning society: that its decisive power be legitimate power. It would actually increase the danger of nonlegitimate power. There are so many corporation managements that competition often prevents concerted political action even in our "economy of monopolistic competition." But there could only be a few union leaders united in one closely knit ring.

Unionism also fails to provide the other prerequisite of a functioning society, the social integration of the individual. For what is the status and function of the member of a unionist society? What social purpose does his life have? And what individual purpose does a unionist society fulfill? A union must of necessity en-force equal conditions in all comparable plants in the same industry. Hence it cannot allow one plant to be-come a community of its own with a functional integra-tion of the worker and his work. It can only protect the worker politically and economically against exploita-tion. But what is its purpose when it dominates and when the union of the exploited workers has become the top dog? There are no answers to these questions; they are unanswerable.

Unionism as a political force collapses as soon as the conditions disappear which the trade-unions have been developed to correct. There is no weaker political and social structure than an established, successful and *arrivé* trade-union system. Politically unionism and unions are strong only so long as they are young, strug-gling against heavy odds and the sacred cause of a fanat-ical minority. As soon as they become big, dominant, and respectable they become flabby. This is due to the character of unionism and of trade-unions as a critique, a corrective, an antibody. If the majority of the workers are organized and the majority of big businesses under union contract, the trade-unions lose all but administrative functions. Owing to the necessarily centralized character of the organization—a few big unions with a few national presidents and secretaries—they can be destroyed without any danger of real opposition. For the threat of the general strike ceases to be a practical one in a country where unionism is no longer a partisan issue but an accomplished fact.

The seemingly strongest, best organized and best managed trade-union organization of our times, the German trade-unions, were captured and destroyed without a struggle. Hitler arrested a handful of union leaders, occupied a few central offices, and confiscated a score of accounts. And the apparently most powerful and most successful trade-union system of industrial Europe had ceased to exist. To bring the business managers under their control was infinitely more difficult for the Nazi régime than to destroy the unions. There were more business managers, they were not as centralized as the unions, and they were needed as technicians. The same thing happened seven years later in France—again a fully unionized country.

Unionism cannot become the basis of a functioning society. But also it cannot become the basis of a powerful political movement. It is in essence only the shadow

of corporation management; and it can neither succeed
the managers nor overcome them.

None of the various short cuts to a functioning industrial society can achieve what they promise. They are
not all futile or wasted. They should all contribute important features to the future—if we succeed in reach-
ing the future free industrial society without a political
revolution or a social collapse, and without the destruction of our social freedom. But the contributions of these
movements and philosophies to the future industrial society will be confined to incidentals and techniques. They
cannot provide a basis.

In this situation in which there are many palliatives
but no remedy it was to be expected that sooner or later
there would be an attempt to make our present industrial nonsociety appear a perfectly functioning society.
This attempt has recently been made by James Burnham in a book which has aroused great interest in this
country.*

Mr. Burnham claims that managerial power is legitimate power. More important, he only said out loud what
a great many managers have been thinking; he does not
see any problem of legitimacy at all. According to him,
the rise of the managers "inevitably" leads to a man-

---

* James Burnham: *The Managerial Revolution* (New York: John
Day, 1941).

agerial society in which the managers will rule. Nazism, Communism and the New Deal appear to him but different "fronts" for the same managerial rule. Insofar as there is any question regarding the title on which this rule will rest, Mr. Burnham assumes that an appropriate ideology will be tailored to measure and sold to the people as, according to him—and to all other Marxists— has been done before in the case of property rights and all preceding titles to legitimate power.

Against this analysis it must first be said that nothing is inevitable in political life, which is the product of man's decisions. An appeal to inevitability is usually an appeal to slaves to accept slavery. It is significant that Mr. Burnham considers it "inevitable" that all industrial countries must go totalitarian.

But Mr. Burnham's analysis is also a perversion of the developments of the last twenty years. The "managerial society" which he forecasts for the future has been our society in the first third of the present century. And it belongs already to the past.

To call Hitlerism and the New Deal "fronts for managerial rule" is absurd. Though they had nothing in common, both régimes attacked managerial power. Nazism made the abolition of managerial power and the assumption of the manager's political functions by the central government one of the mainstays in its attempt to create a functioning industrial society. In the United

States, the attempt to divest management of its social and political power, and to transfer these powers to authorities claiming legitimacy on the basis of majority rule, was the gist of the New Deal's social program.

The people in the industrial countries still accept individual property rights as a basis for legitimate power. This was clearly evidenced in the popular support which Henry Ford received in his fight against unionism and against the New Deal. But there was no such popular support for mere managerial power; General Motors, though on the basis of their record probably more deserving of support, obtained none. In other words, there is simply no evidence for the assumption of Mr. Burnham—and of the managers who applauded him—that actual rule successfully invents its own ideological justification. The opposite is true today, as it has always been true in the past. The exercise of power must be based on an existing and accepted basic principle in order to be legitimate. If there is no such principle, the power becomes despotic and politically unbearable.

No social power can endure unless it is legitimate power. Unless the power in the corporation can be organized on an accepted principle of legitimacy, it will disappear. It will be taken over by a central government —not because the government wants the power but because it will be forced by the people to assume it.

And no society can function unless it integrates the

individual member. Unless the members of the industrial system are given the social status and function which they lack today, our society will disintegrate. The masses will not revolt; they will sink into lethargy; they will flee the responsibility of freedom, which without social meaning is nothing but a threat and a burden. We have only one alternative: either to build a functioning industrial society or to see freedom itself disappear in anarchy and tyranny.

CHAPTER FIVE

THE CHALLENGE AND THE
FAILURE OF HITLERISM

THE emergence of Hitlerism has made the development of a functioning industrial society our most vital, most urgent task. Hitlerism is not only an attempt to create a functioning industrial society—an attempt which nearly succeeded. It is also an attempt to find a new social ideal as basis of society. And it proceeds from the abandonment of the very freedom to achieve which was the goal of the mercantile society and the justification of its social ideal, social institutions and political power.

Viewed as an attempt to create a functioning society, the Nazi party, the many semi-military organizations built around it and, finally, the Nazi Army, at once "make sense" socially. They are the institutions in which Hitlerism has tried to give the individual social status and function. There has been a tendency to see in these institutions nothing but "fronts" to mask the social emptiness of Nazism, or mere disguises for a rearmament drive at a time when Germany did not yet dare to arm openly. There is a great deal of truth in either explanation. One or both of these may have been originally the only purpose the Nazi leaders had in mind when they created their organizations. But whatever the original purpose, these new organizations have become social institutions, and their purpose has become that of integrating the individual member of the industrial system into a society.

In the Nazi organizations the individual is given a status and a function quite independent of the productive process; that is, quite independent of his economic status and function. At least in theory, but also largely in practice, his rank in these organizations is in no way dependent upon his wealth, his income or his status in the old society. The only criteria are political ability, qualities of leadership, and loyalty to the Fuehrer. The Nazi creed of the purpose of the life of the individual is that it be "totally" integrated with the life of the national or racial group. If this purpose were indeed accepted as the basic purpose of individual life, then the Nazi organizations would have succeeded in integrating individual and group in a common purpose—the first criterion of a functioning society.

Actually, the Nazi organizations have been attempting to realize social equality, or at least to offset economic inequality, by giving equal chances in the noneconomic sphere to the economically underprivileged. It has been the practice in all Nazi organizations to give positions of command and authority largely to people who occupy subordinate positions in the economic sphere. Conversely, members of the upper classes have been pointedly assigned to inferior positions in the Nazi hierarchy. In the Nazi units in factories or businesses it is usually an unskilled worker or a junior clerk, often a man formerly unemployed, who is put on top. After working hours he is the boss of the very people whom he has to obey during working hours. When the universities were organized as units in the Nazi system, around 1936 or 1937, it was often the janitor who emerged as unit leader and as the political and social superior of professors and deans. It is standing practice in all Nazi legations and embassies to have a junior clerk occupy the highest political position within the Nazi organization of the embassy. He is the Secret Police representative on the spot who watches over the loyalty of his superiors and who is in direct contact with the authorities at home. He also enjoys direct disciplinary powers over the entire embassy personnel. The ambassador's authority is purely external and confined to the relationship with the foreign government to which he is accredited. Internally an obscure third secretary, press attaché or code clerk is the boss and the direct representative of the Fuehrer. In the same way professors of a university, or vice-presidents of a corporation are in authority only with respect to external relations—toward students, customers, and the public at large. Internally, the power of command has largely been transferred to a party functionary who very often is taken from the ranks of those who have no political or social standing in the economic sphere.

This policy may well have originated in sheer expediency. The unskilled worker become political boss may have been the one person in the whole plant whom the Nazis could trust. He may have been regarded also as completely dependent upon the political power which created him. But Nazi newspapers and publicists have become unanimous in their contempt for rank and status in the economic sphere as something that belongs to the *ancien régime,* to the past. Even though the individual cases may have been due to ad hoc considerations and not to deliberate policy, their cumulative effect has been the creation of a deliberate and conscious social reorientation.

A more serious argument against the attempt to ascribe a deliberate social policy to the Nazis would be that the social policies and programs of Nazism are so confused, so contradictory and so full of hidden and open conflicts of ideas and interests as to make ridiculous the assumption of a social master-plan. There is far less "masterminding," in the Nazi system than the world, impressed by Nazi propaganda, commonly assumes. Especially in the social field, the propaganda impression of great basic concepts is as much a fake front for planless plunging as the propaganda picture of a "monolithic unity" is a cover for very real and very deep conflicts within the party and within the country. The practice of giving rank in the Nazi hierarchy may not have grown out of a consistent and intentional policy, but the result has been that the Nazi organizations have on a large scale given superior rank to those who hold inferior rank in the economic system—and very largely to those who, like the unemployed unskilled worker, had no function and status in economic society.

The basically social meaning of this practice shows in its most direct form in the Nazification of that last bulwark of the old society: the German Army. In the old army, status and function were organized according to the social order of the pre-1914 society. A substantial part of the regular commissions were reserved for the Junkers. But the mercantile ruling class of professional and business men was admitted as reserve officers. Nobody could get a reserve commission unless he came from a "respectable family." There was no mass army in pre-1914 Europe—except the Russian—in which the lower classes were as rigidly excluded from officers' commissions as in the German Army.

Today, according to all reports, there is no army in Europe where promotion from the ranks is more common than in the Nazi Army. Status and function in the

Nazified German Army go according to skill. And the skills which bring a commission to the rank of officer and advancement within the officers' corps are very largely industrial skills: the skills of mechanic and repair man, of foreman and straw boss, of truck driver and production engineer. These are skills which, as a rule, neither the economically privileged classes nor the Junkers possess. These two classes are therefore handicapped in the new Nazi Army. This is largely obscured to the foreign observer. For the commanders on the top whose names are the only ones an American or English newspaper reader is likely to come across are often veterans from the last war and therefore still products of the social selection operating before 1914. But the regimental and divisional officers of today—the commanders of tomorrow—seem to come to an increasing degree from the lower middle classes and the working class. The continuous complaints of the old army hierarchy, that the army is being "proletarized" and that there are "no more gentlemen left in the army," are abundant proof of this.

Of course, this "proletarization" of the army was largely dictated by technological reasons. To repair a tank or to operate a big bomber requires a degree of mechanical skill which cannot be acquired in an old-line cadet academy or in the study of law. Another obvious reason was political expediency. It is essential politi-

cally for the Nazi régime to destroy the only surviving
social group of the old order—the old officers' corps.
But the desire to give those who are economically unequal a compensation in the noneconomic society of the
army was at least as decisive as the opportunist considerations. The so-called "democratization of the army" is
one of the foremost slogans of Nazi propaganda at
home. Over and over again it is repeated: In the new
army rank is given exclusively according to military
and technical skill; status and function in the army no
longer depend upon wealth or birth; true social equality
has been realized in the army.

According to the Nazi creed the party organizations
and the army are the only socially significant and constitutive institutions. They are society per se. The economic sphere is regarded as not only subordinate but
as socially meaningless. It is pictured as socially neutral
in its values, in its ranking and in its stratification. It is
not denied that there is economic inequality, nor that a
very large number of men have no status and no function in the economic sphere. It is simply asserted that it
does not matter socially what happens in the economic
sphere as long as the productive machinery runs
smoothly. The Nazi hierarchy with its party and army
organization is the one sphere in which status and function are social status and social function. Rank in it is

social rank, prestige is social prestige and rewards are social rewards.

The often heard criticism, that nothing really changes if an unemployed worker is put into uniform and appointed a storm-troop leader, is meaningless from the Nazi point of view. This criticism is based upon the obvious fact that the storm-troop leader is as unproductive in his uniform as he was before when he was on relief. There is no economic change. Accordingly, in a society in which social status and function are status and function in the productive process, the change is no change at all. Not so in Nazism where the storm troops are a social institution, whereas the productive system is not. According to Nazism, an outcast has been restored to citizenship in the society and has been given social status and function where he had none before. The criticism that he does not produce any more goods than before would appear to a Nazi perfect nonsense and a complete misunderstanding of the nature of his society.

The *social* meaning of the Nazi organizations is the attempt to integrate into an industrial society the individual living in the industrial system. And in the center of the Nazi *political* system is the attempt to make the decisive power in the industrial system legitimate power. One of the main reasons of the strength of the Nazi economic machine has been the understanding that property rights have ceased to be a basis of power in the industrial system. The Nazis never bothered about the shareholder—legally the owner and controller of modern industrialism. They just by-passed him. While he got his dividends, good care was taken that he pay them out again in taxes or in "voluntary" investments in government bonds. While he retained a part of his legal rights, the political authorities saw to it that he did not exercise them. To "liquidate" the shareholder would have been as disturbing politically as it was easy to paralyze him. Besides, from the Nazi point of view, nothing would have been gained by a nationalization of property; political and social powers in the industrial system do not rest with property but with physical control.

The focus of all Nazi political organization is the physical control of industry. Where formerly the managers wielded this control, the central government now dictates labor policies, production, prices, volume and direction of sales, and profit margin. It has retained the managers as expert advisers on engineering and organizing methods. Of course, it has freed them of shareholders' control and of the necessity to bargain with unions. But it has only freed management from minor limitations on its power in order to impose upon them the total control and absolute rule of a total and absolute government.

The criticism that there can be no freedom under such

complete control of the economic sphere by a total government does not, of course, appear to the Nazis a valid
criticism. They never pretended to establish or to maintain freedom; they have always regarded its abolition
as necessary and desirable. All that matters from the
Nazi point of view is that the decisive power in the
industrial system has been assumed by that organ which,
according to the Nazi creed, is the legitimate holder of
all power: a central government based upon the "Fuehrer's Will" or the "law of the race." In other words, to
say that Nazism is the destruction of freedom—as is,
of course, only too true—in no way disproves the Nazi
claim that their government has legitimate power and
that, therefore, their society is a functioning industrial
society. The attack on Nazism has therefore to start with
a refutation of the Nazi claim that theirs can be a functioning society.

The starting point of Nazi political theory was the
conviction that the modern industrial mass-production
plant is the model for a totalitarian state. Twenty years
ago that was said by the two writers who have influenced
Nazi social policies and theories more than anybody
else: the novelist Ernst Juenger and the romanticist socialist Moeller van den Bruck. The organizations of
Nazism are pre-eminently designed to take hold of, and
to integrate, urban masses. All Nazi organizations in-

cluding the party itself are constructed of small "cells"
—a city block, a factory, a university. This system only
works in a physical environment in which people live
closely together. From the earliest days of the Nazi
movement there have been complaints that the organization does not function in rural surroundings where the
required close supervision and hierarchy of petty bosses
becomes unworkable. The spectacular advance of Nazism began in 1927—long before the Depression—with
the first application of these principles to an industrial
city: Berlin. Before that time Nazism, while supported
by powerful rural and small middle-class elements,
never could organize for large-scale political action. The
model Nazi organization was built in the great industrial Berlin suburb of Siemenstadt where the organization of the workers in the factories—the "factory cell"
—is the basis for the organization of the population
after working hours, and where the factory politician
is at the same time the ward boss.

This may seem to contradict Nazi ideology with its
glorification of the farmers, its *"Lebensraum"* and its
"blood and soil" slogan. Of course, all this cheap Wagnerian pseudo romanticism goes on. It is even probable
that Hitler himself believes in it. But that matters as
little as Columbus' lifelong belief that what he discov-
ered was really the Indies. The reality of Hitlerism is

anything but romantic; it is anything but Wagnerian and it is totally free from any glorification of the farmer or the soil. Actually, in Nazism, the farmer has been made an outcast. The famous "Hereditary Farm Law," which pretends to give the farmer perpetual and secure ownership of his land, really gives the land perpetual and secure ownership of the farmer. It is a return to villeinage under which the farmer resigns his claim to status and function in society in order to have an imaginary protection against society. If—as seemed possible at several stages during the last ten years—the Nazis had decided to collectivize all farms on the Soviet model, it would hardly have made any difference to the social structure of the Nazi system. The Nazi agrarianism is nothing but a stage property—and, even as such, shoddy. The emphasis of the Nazi régime has been from the beginning on the political organization of total industrial production. The real internal enemies of Nazism from the beginning have been the ruling classes of the preindustrial, the mercantile society.*

The concept of man's nature on which Nazism bases

---

* Even Nazi racial anti-Semitism is primarily a means to destroy the representative class of the mercantile society: the upper bourgeoisie of professional men, bankers, merchants, industrialists, etc. The particular historical and social conditions which led to the identification of this class with the Jews and Non-Aryans in Central Europe, and the reasons why racial (as against religious) anti-Semitism meant the actual destruction of this class have been discussed in detail in the chapter "Miracle or Mirage?" in my *End of Economic Man*.

itself is that of Heroic Man. And the purpose of society in which the man of Nazism finds his fulfillment is War and Conquest.

That war is the main purpose of society, the true fulfillment of man's nature and the basic principle of social order and political organization, has certainly been a fundamental conviction of the Nazi leaders and theoreticians from the time when their movement was nothing but one of countless back-parlor conventicles. But to say that Heroic Man became the basis of Nazi society, and war its purpose because Hitler and his lieutenants wanted it so, is far too simple. Actually, there were for many years attempts within the Nazi party and the Nazi leadership to find an alternative basic principle.

But no alternative could do the job of providing a basis for the social integration and the political power of a *totalitarian industrial system*. Only total armament could provide the jobs for the unemployed. Military or semi-military organizations were the only ones in which the individual member of the industrial system could be given status and function independent of economic status and economic function. And only war and the preparation for it enabled the central government to establish complete and direct control of the productive system and to take over the political and social power wielded before by the industrial managers and the union leaders.

Most people probably believe that it is this creed of war and conquest which has made Nazism the world danger which it is today. Actually, it is this very creed which may have prevented Nazism from conquering the world. Most people would also think that this single-minded devotion to war and conquest is the main source of the strength of the Nazis. But it is probably their greatest and their fatal weakness. And only too many people believe that Nazism would have been harmless but for its religion of militarism. But it is this very creed of war and conquest which will ultimately prove to have been the factor that defeated Nazism. That Hitlerism could find no other basis for industrial society than war and conquest may eventually turn out to have been the salvation for those who hate and repudiate Nazism and all it stands for. Far from being the source of the Nazis' strength, their basic purpose of war and conquest is the root of their real failure. Far from being the greatest threat to freedom, it may well be the one thing that has given us a chance to work for a free industrial society.

Because the Nazis could not find any other basis for their society than war and conquest, theirs has not become a functioning society. No people in the Western world—not even the Germans—have been willing to accept war as the ultimate, the highest aim of society. Consequently, the attempted integration of the individual into society through status and function in the Nazi organizations has failed to become a valid functioning integration. The individual has not accepted war and conquest as the basic aims of life—neither of his own, individual life nor of the life of the group.

This failure of Nazism to develop an industrial society on any basis but war and conquest, and with any other concept of man's nature than that of Heroic Man, has given those of us who believe in freedom a chance to fight for it. More, it has rallied to the cause of freedom millions who had already given up freedom—except for empty lip service. There is little doubt that the great masses in the industrial system—at least in Europe—could have been persuaded to abandon freedom and to accept slavery. All they asked for was security. The famous, or rather infamous, declaration of a group of French Socialists just before the outbreak of the war, that they would rather be Hitler's slaves than fight a war, only said aloud what millions of others were thinking. And the English newspaper writer who, after Munich, declared that the Czechs ought to be grateful as they were now able to live in peace and security instead of in constant dread of war, was also no isolated phenomenon.

Had Nazism been able to find any other basis for slavery than war and conquest, its totalitarian revolution might have swept Europe without encountering any resistance at all. Whenever the Nazis pretended to consider another basis for totalitarianism than war and conquest, they found immediate response in other countries. There was a desperate hope among the industrial masses, rich and poor, right and left alike—to be given a secure and nonmilitant basis for slavery. In France, the Nazi propaganda slogan of a total state based on the pseudo romanticism of the Youth Movement converted many, especially on the Left, to "collaboration" with Hitler and Hitlerism. In England, the hope of a Nazism based on the "body beautiful" even found expression in a feeble but government-sponsored imitation, the Keep Fit campaign which was fortunately speedily buried under the ruins of Munich.

These may appear very minor aberrations of a hysterical and mentally unbalanced period. But as symptoms they are important. They show the attraction which Hitler's totalitarianism would have had upon the industrial countries of Europe had he but been able to offer security as the basis of his slavery.

But Nazism could only offer war as the basis of slavery. The peoples of Europe were not willing to accept war and conquest as the basic purpose of society. They were thus forced by the Nazis themselves to repudiate slavery. The people who, above all, wanted security even at the price of freedom, now have to fight for their freedom. Hitler himself—nobody else—has unwittingly and unwillingly given freedom a meaning and a value it had all but lost.

This does not mean that a defeat of Hitlerism will inevitably bring about a free society. On the contrary, it is certain that this defeat by itself will not even create a functioning industrial society, let alone one which is also free. After a war as destructive and as uprooting as this, the people will above all demand a functioning society. They will be even more ready than they were before the war, to sacrifice freedom, if this should appear to be the necessary price for a comprehensible, meaningful and functioning order. The greatest danger today is that we shall defeat Hitler's totalitarianism of war only in order to replace it by one of peace and security. All the schemes for postwar order which place the security of permanent peace above all other goals— such as, for instance, that of a world superstate—come dangerously close to abandoning freedom and to a to- talitarianism which would be all the more threatening as it would be much harder to attack, morally and physically, than Hitler's.

We cannot expect a free industrial society as an inevi- table and logical consequence of victory. Victory is only the first condition. But there is at least a good chance to- day that we shall succeed. It is certain that a functioning industrial society of the Western peoples will grow out of this war—if there is to be a West. It is for the basis and structure of this society that the war is being fought. Precisely because the very foundations of our society are the stakes in this war it should be possible to make this functioning industrial society a free society.

So far in this book we have tried to answer the question: What is a functioning society and what is wanted to give the industrial system a functioning society? Now we shall have to answer the equally basic question: What is a free society?

CHAPTER SIX

FREE SOCIETY AND FREE
GOVERNMENT

SHORTLY before the United States entered this war the City of New York staged a "freedom rally" under the slogan: "It's fun to be free." It is unlikely that the choice of this slogan was dictated by anything more profound than the conviction of those great thinkers, our modern advertising and propaganda sages, that a "consumers' demand" and a "market" can be created for ideas in the same way, by the same means, and to the same end as for lipstick. Yet as a symptom the incident was important. It illustrates the confusion and the loss of political sense and understanding which is the greatest weakness of the free countries today. To say that it is fun to be free comes close to a repudiation of the real freedom. The mob of Imperial Rome at least never pretended that circuses and freedom were identical. It had the courage to admit that it preferred circuses.

Freedom is not fun. It is not the same as individual happiness, nor is it security or peace and progress. It is not the state in which the arts and sciences flourish. It is also not good, clean government or the greatest welfare of the greatest number. This is not to say that freedom is inherently incompatible with all or any of these values —though it may be and sometimes will be. But the essence of freedom lies elsewhere. It is responsible choice. Freedom is not so much a right as a duty. Real freedom is not freedom from something; that would be license. It is freedom to choose between doing or not doing something, to act one way or another, to hold one belief or the opposite. It is never a release and always a responsibility. It is not "fun" but the heaviest burden laid on man: to decide his own individual conduct as well as the conduct of society, and to be responsible for both decisions.

Unless there are decision and responsibility there is no freedom. There may be happiness, security, peace, and progress. But it would be the happiness and peace of that most despotic tyranny, that of Dostoevsky's Grand Inquisitor who did not even leave to his subjects the right to be unhappy or the decision whether they wanted to live in peace and security or not.

We know that freedom is not a "primitive" state of human existence. Primitive society everywhere and at any time tries to eliminate both choice and responsibility —the first through a rigid system of customs, taboos, and traditions; the second through magic ritual. Nor does man instinctively incline toward freedom. The "well-adjusted" person will try instinctively to run away from the burden of choice and the weight of responsibility. If there is one statement that is more contrary to the facts than that man is born free, it is that man will choose freedom if only left to himself. Psychologically, the Grand Inquisitor of Dostoevsky's legend was certainly right when he maintained against Jesus that man would rather be a happy slave than a responsible freeman.

Yet freedom is the "natural" state of human existence. It is neither the original condition of man historically nor his instinctive or emotional choice psychologically. But it is natural, necessary and inevitable metaphysically—though only under one philosophical concept of man's nature. Freedom is not only possible, it is inevitable on the basis of the belief that every single human being has to choose between good and evil. No man, no group of men can escape this choice; for no man nor any group of men can ever be in possession of absolute knowledge, absolute certainty, absolute truth, or absolute right.

The only basis of freedom is the Christian concept of man's nature: imperfect, weak, a sinner, and dust destined unto dust; yet made in God's image and responsible for his actions. Only if man is conceived as basically and immutably imperfect and impermanent, is freedom philosophically both natural and necessary.

And only if he is seen as basically and inescapably responsible for his acts and decisions, in spite of his imperfection and impermanence, is freedom politically possible as well as required. Any philosophy which claims perfection for human beings denies freedom; and so does a philosophy that renounces ethical responsibility.

An assumption of human perfection or of a known or knowable process of human perfectibility leads inescapably to tyranny and totalitarianism. Freedom is impossible as soon as only one man out of the whole of humanity is assumed perfect or more nearly perfect than his fellow men. For the assumption of human perfection or perfectibility renounces man's right and duty to choose.

The perfect man is in possession of absolute truth. He is at least closer to it than his fellow men; or he knows an infallible method to reach it. But if absolute truth is known or knowable there is no justification for doubt or for choice. There can be no freedom against absolute truth, no opposition against absolute right. To choose differently when truth is known, to decide for oneself when right has spoken, is at best folly. If stubbornly persisted in, it becomes wickedness and treason.

Any man assumed perfect or perfectible is not only entitled to absolute rule, but has a moral obligation to assume the rule. He must disregard criticism, opposition and dissenting counsel. Since he, and he alone, knows what is good for his subjects, he is in duty bound to suppress all their expressions of the freedom of choice and decision. Torture and concentration camps for dissenters, the firing squad for opponents, and a secret police spying on everybody's words, deeds, and thoughts are perfectly legitimate from the point of view of the ruler who claims or is accorded perfection or perfectibility. For those who do not accept his dictates repudiate truth deliberately. They willingly and wittingly choose evil.

All this is just as true if we substitute a group of men for the one infallible ruler. No other government but tyranny is possible on the basis of the assumption that one man or one group of men is right or likely to be right. And no tyranny could be more oppressive or more complete than that based on the claim to absolute truth and absolute right. "Ye shall be as gods, knowing good and evil" has forever been the advice of the Serpent.

There can also be no freedom if man is not held responsible for his decisions between good and evil, true and false. Without responsibility there can only be anarchy and a war of all against all.

To deny responsibility is to deny that there is an absolute good or an absolute truth. But freedom becomes meaningless if there is only relative good or relative evil. Decisions would have no ethical meaning; they would be nothing but an arbitrary guess without consequences.

There are many people today who are perfectly willing to admit that no man can claim possession of absolute truth or absolute reason. The basis for their admission is, however, not the imperfection of man but the nonexistence of absolutes. They do not doubt man's perfection; they doubt God's existence. Hence they deny that there is any ethical responsibility for decisions. And they deny freedom fully as much as the man who says: "I am God." The relativist and the pragmatist say in effect that the decision ought to go to the stronger; for everything is equally socially workable. Whoever can make his view prevail is therefore right. On this basis there can be no reason why the freedom of the weaker should be protected, or why he should even be allowed to express his dissenting opinion.

It may be said that freedom is possible only on the assumption that in a conflict of fundamentals either side is likely to be wrong and certain to be at least partially wrong. If one side is assumed to be likely to be right, there can be no freedom. The other side could not demand a right to advocate an opinion which dissents from what is presumed to be the truth. It would not even have a right to have such an opposing view. Also, in order to have freedom, it must be assumed that there is absolute truth and absolute reason—though forever beyond man's grasp. Otherwise there could be no responsibility; without responsibility there would be no reason other than material interests to have any opinion at all, and no right to voice it except the right of the stronger.

Freedom is the strength arising out of inherent human weakness. It is the skepticism based upon profound faith. If *one* man were perfectly good there could be no freedom as he would be entitled to absolute rule. And if one man were perfectly evil he would inevitably possess himself of absolute rule. If *all* men were perfectly good or perfectly evil, there need be no freedom since there never would be any doubt about any decision. It is only because no man is perfectly good or perfectly evil that there is a justification of freedom. And only because it is everybody's personal duty to strive for the good is there a need for freedom.

Freedom, as we understand it, is inconceivable outside and before the Christian era. The history of freedom does not begin with Plato or Aristotle. Neither could have visualized any rights of the individual against society, although Aristotle came closer than any man in the pre-Christian era to the creed that man is inherently imperfect and impermanent. Nor does the history of freedom begin with those Athenian "totalitarian liberals," the Sophists who denied all responsibility of the individual because they denied the existence of absolutes.

The roots of freedom are in the Sermon on the Mount and in the Epistles of St. Paul; the first flower of the tree of liberty was St. Augustine. But after two thousand years of development from these roots we still have trouble in understanding that freedom is a question of decision and responsibility, not one of perfection and efficiency. In other words, we still confuse only too often the Platonic question: what is the best government? with the Christian question: what is a free society?

It is impossible to define freedom in other than individual terms—as a right and duty which can neither be taken from the individual nor be evaded or delegated by him. But this does not mean that freedom has no social meaning. There has been no greater and no more fatal mistake than that of the early Lutheran theologians who declared the social sphere to be irrelevant, indifferent and outside individual decision and responsibility. Freedom is destroyed if it is confined to "inner freedom," and responsibility to one's private life. Individual freedom requires a free society for its fulfillment. Yet there can be no freedom of society against the individual. The right of society to protect itself against the individual is one limitation of freedom, not freedom itself. There can be no freedom of the majority against the minority, no freedom of the stronger against the weaker. It is important to protect and preserve society. But it has nothing to do with freedom, except as restriction on it. The legitimate rights of society, of the organized group, of the majority against the individual, are the one limit to freedom. Its other limit is license—the free individual choice without responsibility. To be "free" to choose between ice cream and plum pudding for dessert is not freedom, since no responsibility attaches to the decision. Freedom is thus forever contained within, and limited by, those two states of un-freedom: the one in which there is no individual decision, and the other in which there is no individual responsibility. The encroachment of the one or the other is thus forever a threat to freedom. Too little individual decision on the one hand, too little individual responsibility on the other —are the end of freedom.

Man has the same right and the same duty to decide responsibly on the actions of the society of which he is a member as on his individual actions. He is not only his brother's keeper; man is his brother's brother, and as much a member of the family as the brother. He cannot on the assumption of man's nature, on which freedom is based, deny responsibility for the group of which he is a member. He also cannot evade the responsibility by shifting the decision to other shoulders—neither to those of an absolute monarch nor to a parliamentary majority. And no group can deny the individual the right to participate in the decisions.

The political and social conclusions from the freedom of the individual is self-government, self-government as a right and as a duty of the individual. If there is no individual decision in the self-government, it is only a sham. But it is just as much a sham and a camouflage for tyranny if there is no individual responsibility. There must be active, responsible, and spontaneous participation of the individual in the government as his government, in its decisions as his decisions, in its burdens as his burdens. Political freedom is neither easy nor automatic, neither pleasant nor secure. It is the responsibility of the individual for the decisions of society as if they were his own decisions—as in moral truth and accountability they indeed are.

Freedom is an organizing principle of social life. It is not a social or political institution. Free societies with the most widely divergent basic institutions are conceivable and possible. But the institutions must always be organized by and for the responsible decision of the members.

Freedom is a purely formal principle. It always requires a concrete statement about what type of human activity is to be realized freely or what aim of society is to be fulfilled in freedom. There is no conflict between the concept of man as free and the concept of man as Spiritual Man or Economic Man. Any substantial concept of man can be made the basis of a free or of an unfree society. Freedom can be the organizing principle for any kind of society. But a society is free only if it organizes its basic beliefs in freedom. That socially decisive sphere in which society seeks the fulfillment of its fundamental aims must be organized on the basis of responsible, individual decision.

It is most important to realize that political and social freedom is freedom in the socially constitutive sphere— the sphere in which the values are the social values of a society, the rewards the social rewards, the prestige the social prestige, and the ideals the social ideals. In one society this will be the economic sphere; in another the religious; in a third, for instance in the Germany of the nineteenth century, the cultural sphere. Social and political freedom is thus not an absolute. If the socially constitutive sphere of a society is organized on the basis of the responsible decision of the individual, we have a free society—even if nothing else in that society should be free. If the socially constitutive sphere in a society is not free, the whole society is unfree; yet everything else may be completely uncontrolled and a matter of social indifference and individual license.

That freedom is an organizing principle of social life is one of the most important points in the theory and practice of politics. The failure to understand it has been responsible for a great many misunderstandings and mistakes. The Western world, for instance, found it almost impossible to understand that capitalist economic freedom was not freedom for the Balkan peasant. The national states which were organized in southeastern Europe after 1918 expected to create a functioning society by adopting the mercantile capitalism and the free market and money economy of the nineteenth-century West. But to the peasants who constitute the great majority in the Balkans, the economic sphere was not a socially constitutive sphere, and economic values were not social values. They had no ideal of economic progress and no belief that freedom and justice could or should be realized in the economic sphere. Their society was tribal and religious. Economic freedom to the Balkan peasants simply meant insecurity, the tyranny of the international market and the compulsion to choose and to act as a responsible individual in a sphere in which they saw neither need for, nor justification of, choice and responsibility. The Balkan peasants value and cherish freedom more perhaps than anybody else in Europe; yet economic freedom was only a threat to them.

This also explains the meaning and importance of political freedom—in the narrow formal sense of the word "political" in which it is confined to the sphere of organized government. There can be no free society unless it has a considerable degree of political freedom.

But formal political freedom and free government do not constitute a free society in themselves. They are an essential condition of freedom but not its fulfillment.

The political sphere is never in itself the socially constitutive sphere—except, perhaps, in a society engaged in total war. Political institutions are the mechanism through which power is organized for the fulfillment of society's purposes and decisions. Without free political institutions a free society could not be effectual; it could not translate its decisions into social reality. It could not institutionalize freedom in the form of responsible self-government. But if there is no freedom in the socially constitutive sphere the most perfectly free political institutions could not establish a free society. They would have nothing to do and would degenerate for lack of function.

Freedom rests on ethical decisions. But the political sphere deals with power. And power is only a tool and in itself ethically neutral. It is not a social purpose and not an ethical principle.

Individually, power may well be the goal of personal ambition. But socially it is a servant; its organization is only a means to a social end. The role of power in society may be likened to the role of money in an economy. Money may well be the goal of an individual's economic activity. Yet if the economy is viewed as a whole, money does not exist. It is simply a means to distribute the goods internally among the individual members of the economic systems; socially, the only product of an economy is the goods. Similarly, power distributes rank and determines relations within a society; it is a means of internal organization. But the end of society is always an ethical purpose.

This thesis would probably be generally accepted. But it leads to conclusions which contradict some of the most popular beliefs. It is today almost an axiom that political action or constitutional legislation are socially omnipotent. But if formal political freedom is only the condition and not the realization of freedom, purely political action cannot create freedom nor increase it to any decisive extent—once there is the necessary minimum of free government. And a free society cannot be legislated into existence—though it can be legislated out of existence if the necessary minimum of free government is politically destroyed. The major task in the building of a free society thus lies in the field of social institutions.

To give a specific example: The respect and reverence for the Constitution in the United States is a social phenomenon which could not have been produced by legislative enactment. But it is far more important and effective for America's free society than the actual provisions of the Constitution themselves, excellent though they are. Without the greatness of the Constitution, the reverence might never have become the moral force it is. But without this reverence the excellence of the Constitution would have been of no avail. The respect and reverence for the Constitution did by no means follow automatically from its excellence. There have been constitutions as good or perhaps even better in theory which never became social institutions and which, consequently, failed completely to safeguard freedom. The Constitution of the German Republic from 1919 to 1933 is a case in point.

The Founding Fathers deserve all the admiration given them for their work. But their great achievement might have been in vain without the great presidents of the "Virginia Dynasty," without John Marshall, and without Lincoln. It is therefore a real danger that we today have come rather close to forgetting that freedom rests upon beliefs and social institutions and not upon laws. If we want to have a free society, we must learn again that the formal act of legislative enactment does not create or determine institutional structure, social beliefs, and human nature.

How much free government and formal political freedom are needed as the minimum for a free society, is a vital question. But it can hardly be decided theoretically or in terms applicable to every type of society.

We have learned that the old controversy between monarchical and republican forms of government has nothing to do with freedom, which is equally possible and can be equally destroyed under either.

A free society may be possible with far less free government and far less formal political freedom than the halcyon days of 1919 or 1927 would have regarded as a minimum. At least, by comparison with the modern unfree totalitarian society, the Imperial Germany of 1880 appears definitely a free society. The very limited degree of formal political freedom enjoyed by the Germans of the middle nineteenth century was apparently enough to make possible a very real and very considerable freedom in the economic and cultural spheres. And these were the socially constitutive spheres in German mid-Victorian society. The people in the Nazi-conquered countries—and in Germany too—would need only a fraction of their former political freedom to overthrow the Nazi tyranny and to rebuild a free society. And both the Nazi and Bolshevik secret police act on the assumption that one grain of the yeast of political freedom would spoil a ton of totalitarian dough.

If formal political freedom is only a prerequisite of a free society but not its fulfillment, there are large areas in social life in which no freedom can meaningfully exist. For freedom is responsible choice; and there are spheres in every culture and in every society in which there is either no choice or no responsibility for the choice. Because freedom is an ethical principle of social choice, it has little or nothing to do with those two great areas of human activity and satisfaction: the technical one, in which there is no ethical choice; and the area of social indifference, in which no responsibility attaches to decisions. Only the socially constitutive sphere can be free or unfree; for only in this sphere is there both choice and responsibility.

It is obviously not an ethical or political question whether a right angle has ninety or ninety-five degrees, whether a devaluation of the dollar will raise commodity prices, whether sugar production in Australia would be possible or profitable, or whether a railroad from New York to Washington should be laid along one route or the other. These are technical questions. There can be a great deal of discussion about them, a great deal of disagreement among the experts, a tremendous amount of agitation and "free discussion." These questions constitute the great bulk of the daily problems of an individual and of a society. But to everyone there is one correct answer. What is correct today may be made incorrect tomorrow by an advance in our knowledge or experience or by changes in the facts; but at any given time and place there is one optimum. And this optimum is provable, measurable, demonstrable; in other words, it is objectively correct. It may be a mathematical proof, or a proper accounting method, engineering, or profitability—any of the tests of success which the pragmatists call "workability." Always there is one correct answer —and that means that the human will does not enter. Without human will, however, there can be no choice. And without choice there is no freedom. The whole technical or scientific field is, in other words, ethically neutral; and freedom, like all other basic values, is an ethical value.*

This means, on the one hand, that the attempts to create a "Marxist" biology or a "Nazi" physics are as much nonsense as the talk about a "democratic" psychology. Such scientific or technical questions as the chemical composition of the atmosphere of the planets, the greatest amount of tax that can be raised from the smallest number of tax payers, the effects of a new drug, and so on, are concerned with measurable and demonstrable facts. They furnish the means to realize political, social, or cultural decisions. But they are not decisions themselves. They answer the question: how can we reach a given aim? But the basic decisions are decisions about aims. We have to choose what is desirable; we have to determine the greater good or the lesser evil in the case

---

* I am fully aware that this is a denial of the existence of "scientific truth"; there can be only scientific correctness.

of conflicting aims. We have to decide what sacrifice we are willing to make for a certain achievement, and at what point the sacrifice outweighs the advantages. But the scientist, the engineer, the economist, the expert, are not concerned at all with these political problems. Their work does in no way determine the basic decisions which are value, that is, ethical decisions. Their answers are equally valid whether society is free or unfree.

There is no real decision, no real alternative, no question of good or evil in the field of techniques. But there is no social responsibility in those spheres of social and individual life which are socially indifferent. Whether an American in the 1930's belonged to the Baptists or the Methodists, whether he was a Mason, a Rotarian, or a Shriner, whether he went to Harvard or to North Dakota Teachers College or quit school at sixteen—all these may have been momentous decisions for the individual himself. But no social responsibility attached to them. They were decisions in a sphere of social indifference. The so-called freedom of decision in these spheres is not freedom at all: it is permissible license. The so-called tolerance in these spheres is not tolerance at all, but indifference. Tolerance for your neighbor's opinions and actions not only presupposes that you must consider him wrong; it also means that you must consider his actions or opinions important. They must be in a sphere which matters morally or socially. To tolerate something that does not matter is neither a virtue nor a vice.

This does not mean that indifference is bad. It only means that it has no direct bearing on the question of freedom. A society can be free yet lay down the most rigid rules of behavior in the socially not constitutive sphere. Victorian England would be one example. And a society would be unfree which permitted absolute license in the socially indifferent spheres, but no responsible decision in the socially constitutive sphere; this was, for instance, the structure of the empires of antiquity.

It is one of the oldest and most hotly debated questions of politics whether a rigid code or complete indifference in the socially indifferent spheres is more conducive or less dangerous to freedom. It is the debate between authoritarianism, or collectivism, and individualism. Much is to be said for each side. Up to a point the argument is correct that too much rigidity in the indifferent spheres tends to undermine the freedom of decision in the socially constitutive sphere. But the opposite argument is also true within limits, that too much license in the indifferent spheres undermines the responsibility in the socially constitutive sphere.

It must be realized, however, that the issue between authoritarianism and individualism is an issue under freedom—or unfreedom—and not a discussion about freedom itself.

To sum up: A free society is one in which the socially constitutive sphere is organized on the principle of the responsible decision of the members of the society. A free society is possible only if man is seen as basically and inherently imperfect and imperfectible—yet responsible for not being perfect or perfectible. There can be no freedom if one man or one group of men—however large or small—is assumed to be inherently perfect or perfectible. Its claim to perfection or perfectibility is a claim to absolute rule.

There can also be no freedom if a man-made absolute is set up as the one and exclusive goal of human endeavor, or as the one and exclusive rule of individual or social conduct. The man-made absolute may be peace or war, economic progress or security, the Nordic Race or the greatest happiness of the greatest number. Each of these must destroy freedom if set up as The Absolute.

Every man-made absolute is a flight from freedom. It denies choice in favor of a determinism under which men act "inevitably." It denounces responsibility for a tyranny under which any action is justified if it conforms to the commands or demands of the absolute ruler with his absolute truth. On the other hand, freedom is possible only if the existence of true absolutes is assumed as certain; otherwise, there can be no responsibility.

Against the idealists who set up as absolute and exclusive their own concepts and ideals, the defenders of freedom must always be realists. But against the realists, positivists, functionalists, pragmatists, relativists, etc., who deny the existence of beliefs and ideals, the defenders of freedom must always be idealists. For freedom is in meaning and essence dualistic. It is based on the polarity between man's imperfection and his responsibility. Without this basic faith there can be no freedom, whatever the laws and the constitution of a society.

Freedom is not a supreme goal. It is not a goal at all but an organizing principle. It is not a priori. It is a conclusion from the Christian dogma of man's nature; the right of choice and the responsibility for it are truly a prioris. Freedom, in other words, is not a concrete institutional form. It is a faith—a faith in man's being at the same time a "proud and yet a wretched thing."

2.

If freedom is possible only on the assumption that man is inherently imperfect and imperfectible, it can exist only under organized government. The absence of government—the utopia of the anarchists—can never be freedom. Anarchy is a state in which the perfectly good and the perfectly wise can live, and in which the perfectly evil must live. Angels do not need a government and devils cannot organize one. Neither of them could or need be free. Hobbes's famous foundation of government upon a contract between perfectly evil men engaged in perpetual civil war is a non sequitur. The conclusion from his assumptions regarding human nature should have been that the war of all against all would go on until there is either only one master with all the rest slaves, or only one man alive with all the rest killed. But there is no warrant in Hobbes's scheme of human nature for the sudden conversion of the human brutes to that moderation and reasonableness which leads them to accept a government. The argument that the reasonably certain expectancy of one slice of bread is preferable to the desperate gamble for the whole loaf has never converted greed or lust for power.

The imperfect, however, must have a government because they can and must be free. They must have objective rules, they must have authority, they must have a final arbiter and they must have organized force to give sanction to the rules and social decisions. Organized government is both the sign of man's weakness and imperfection and the means to convert this weakness into the strength of freedom.

That man needs an organized government is another way of saying that he needs an organized society. Organized government is a necessary part—though by no means the whole—of society. To be free, a government must, however, be a great deal more than just legally and politically organized. It must above all be limited, both as to the extent and the exercise of its power. It must be responsible. And it must be substantially self-government.

Each of these demands follows directly from the assumption regarding the nature of man on which alone freedom can be based. No man, however elected or selected, can be perfect. Hence, no man can be allowed to rule absolutely; whatever the government, there must be limits to its powers beyond which it cannot go without becoming a despotism.

The old demand that government acts be public and according to definite rules has the same source. If the government is not bound to formal rules of procedure, there would be no barrier against arbitrariness. Hence one of the greatest safeguards of freedom has been the judicial review of administrative acts in Anglo-American constitutional law and practice. That administrative officers and administrative agencies are accountable and responsible to the law courts for their official acts is perhaps the most successful institutional limitation on bureaucratic omnipotence. Judicial supervision of administrative agencies may actually be more important as a safeguard of freedom than the justly celebrated right of the American courts to review legislative acts. At least government in England did not become arbitrary, though the English courts can control only administrative acts and cannot set aside Acts of Parliament. But on the Continent of Europe administrative arbitrariness has been a severe threat to freedom. Even where there were special administrative courts dispensing a special administrative code, bureaucracy could not be limited and controlled effectively. And this administrative omnipotence undermined self-government far more than the lack of judicial control of the legislative. This was particularly true of France where administrative acts are held to be outside ordinary law—in contrast to the Anglo-American subordination of administration to the courts.

The demand that government be a "government of laws and not of men" is legalistic nonsense if taken literally. Government is necessarily in the hands of men. It is necessarily concerned with decisions. It is necessarily "political." It deals with matters in which assertion stands against assertion, interest against interest, creed against creed—with no infallible or automatic criterion which is best. There is no greater mistake than the attempt to take the politics out of government. If it is done by making a civil service bureaucracy omnipotent and by entrusting political decisions to the expert selected by the merit system of competitive examinations, it leads not only to the government of the least fit but straight to the tyranny of the printed form. And there is nothing more despotic than bureaucratic rules made absolute.

The basic decisions of government—the substance of politics—cannot be made subject to automatic rules; there would be no decision left. But it is equally true that the forms of the decision, the techniques and the modus in which a free government exercises its power, have to be predictable, public, and subject to some impersonal rule—in other words, limited in their exercise by objective rules of procedure.

The demands that free government be responsible, and that it be substantially self-government, are more or less overlapping. Both are based upon the assumption that man has a responsibility for his decisions which he can neither evade nor delegate. An irresponsible government would be a government which has taken the burden of the decision off the shoulders of the citizens. It would make little difference whether the government is irresponsible because it has arrogated to itself irresponsible power, or because such power has been delegated to it. And the moral responsibility of the individual for the acts of his government is only very incompletely realized by the formal responsibility of the government to the citizens. To make a government a free government the active responsible participation of the citizens in the government is needed. No government can be free in which the citizens do not assume voluntarily the burden of self-government.

3.

Are free government and majority rule compatible? The almost automatic response of the Western world to the question today would be that the two are synonymous. Free government and majority rule are commonly used as freely interchangeable terms. Actually, majority rule is no more identical with free government than are minority or one-man rule. Popular government is compatible with freedom. Under very stringent conditions and limitations it is the best instrument for the realization of freedom. On the other hand, majority government can be incompatible with, and hostile to, freedom and free government. And the concept of majority rule popularly accepted today in the Western world is absolutely and diametrically opposed to freedom and a direct attack upon free government.

Consciously or unconsciously, almost all modern doctrines of popular government start from the premise that the majority decides what is right or wrong, or that its decision creates right. At least, the majority is held more likely to be in possession of reason and truth than the minority. In other words, there is an assumption that the numerical majority is either perfection or nearer to perfection than the minority. In a more extreme—and more usual—form the majority is simply identified with absolute truth and absolute right. What the majority decides to be right is right because the majority decides it is. Further appeal is impossible; indeed, this maxim has been proclaimed as an axiom and as incontrovertible.

We are not interested here in the logical, philosophical or metaphysical implications of a theory which bases a quality: truth, upon a quantity: majority. We are concerned only with the question of practical politics: Is such a majority-rule theory compatible with a free government and a free society? The answer is undoubtedly: No. The majority principle as it is commonly accepted today is a despotic, a tyrannical, an unfree principle.

There could be no right of opposition against the majority if the majority either finds or creates right, truth, or goodness. The majority is the law. It is assumed to be either perfect or closer to perfection than the minority. As soon as it has been determined what fifty-one per cent of the people want, the other forty-nine per cent would have the moral duty to climb on the band wagon and join the majority. It may be theoretically possible under the majoritarian assumption to use free discussion, free speech, and other forms of doubt and dissent before the majority has spoken. But once the will of the

majority has been established, there could not be a justification even for the expression of a doubt or of dissent.
And in reality not even the limited freedom before majority decision is practically possible under the majoritarian assumption. The absolute majority of today will
at once perpetuate itself and will lay down final rules
for all time to come. And how could it be stopped? If
the majority has reason or right by virtue of being a
majority, how and why should it be limited?

Under the majoritarian assumption as it is commonly
held today, only the majority can have rights and duties.
Yet freedom is a right and a duty of the minority and
the individual, independent from, and against, the rights
of the majority. Even the most absolutist majoritarian
acknowledges that; he instinctively talks of individual
freedom, civil liberties, and minority rights. There is
really no room in his creed for individual freedom and
responsibility, or for civil liberties. Yet most present-
day majoritarians think, though mistakenly, that their
belief represents freedom; and they are subjectively
sincere in their protest that they want to strengthen civil
liberties and minority rights.

There is therefore a basic conflict between the objective consequences of the belief of the modern majoritarian and his emotions—a conflict typical of the liberal.
And the liberal parties have spent much time and in-

genuity on attempts to resolve the conflict. The best they can do, however, is to demand that the majority restrain itself voluntarily, observe civil liberties, and grant protection for minorities. But in theory as well as in practice such self-restraint is both insufficient and impractical.

In the first place, such self-limitation cannot create even the barest minimum of freedom. Minority protection and guarantees of civil liberties ensure only a negative freedom: the absence of unrestrained majority tyranny. But they give the individual neither choice nor responsibility; they are not positive freedom. They are vital, and, where they are not safeguarded, freedom and responsible self-government are impossible. But they still withhold from the individual the responsible participation in government which is both his right and his duty.

Secondly—and more importantly—individual rights and civil liberties cannot be maintained or justified under the modern doctrine of majority rule, whatever the intention of the liberal. If the majority finds or creates right and reason, can any minority, any dissident, be protected or even tolerated? And how would any restriction of majority rule be inalienable, permanent, and absolute? The majority would always have the right to withdraw these voluntary concessions. At best, modern majoritarian theory and practice can regard the rights and liberties of the individual as polite but meaningless concessions to ancient superstition. But sooner or later these rights and liberties must come to be regarded as reactionary barriers against the will of the people. They must appear as unjustified privileges of the few against the many, built and operated only by private pressure groups and interests. It will always be those rights and liberties, which are really safeguards of individual freedom, that will most likely be attacked in the name of majority and progress. For they will be the ones that come into conflict with the majority will. True freedom, true inalienable rights, and true civil liberties cannot possibly be maintained under a creed that bases the right of the majority to rule on the claim of the majority to be right or more nearly right than the minority. Modern majoritarian doctrine is completely incompatible with freedom.

That the rule of the absolute majority is tyrannical has been a dogma of political thinking since the earliest days. But the usual conclusion of the reactionary—that monarchy or oligarchy are preferable—is as untenable as the opposite modern view of the majority-rule democrats. The counterargument for monarchy or oligarchy has never been concerned with freedom; it has always been that monarchy and oligarchy are *better* governments. We have here the most blatant example of the confusion between Christian politics concerned with free government, and Aristotelian politics concerned with the best government. All our theoretical and practical discussion of politics suffers from the fact that arguments about freedom are supported or opposed by arguments about the best government and vice versa.

It must be realized that the classic discussion about the best government denies freedom—tacitly but definitely. Freedom is possible only if it is firmly believed that there is no such thing as a "best government"—not even a "better government." Freedom is possible only if no one particular set of rulers—selected or elected one particular way—is assumed better or best. If they are regarded as the best there can be no right of dissent and opposition against them, no choice for the citizen, no responsibility for the individual who would have done his duty by submitting to the superior wisdom of the wiser and better government. Those concerned with freedom will frankly admit that one particular free government may be a much less "good" government than one particular unfree one. All they have to say is that the argument is not relevant to the issue. They will also admit that that government is best in which the best rule. They will only deny that there is any predictable or knowable way to pick the best.

This, far from being an attack on democracy, actually strengthens it. We eliminate the weakest point in the democratic creed if we regard the question of the best government as something human beings can neither answer nor solve in any generally applicable and permanently valid manner. For we can then drop the contention that election by the majority is the most rational method of selecting the *best* man. No other point in the traditional majority rule doctrine has drawn the enemy's fire so persistently and with so much reason. It is simply an untenable and really a ridiculous proposition. But the difficulty disappears when it is realized that we are not talking about the best government and the selection of the best rulers, but about free government and the realization of self-government. We can admit—as is only too obvious—that election by the majority in no way guarantees the selection of the wise, the just, and the best. But the same is true of any other method. It would be just as good or just as bad—how good or how bad depends upon the men who run it at any given time or place. For there is no definite and definable way to select the wise and the best. What matters is whether election by majority vote comes nearer to being a realization of free government than any other method or not.

There have been monarchies which were better governments than democracies, democracies which were better governments than monarchies, and oligarchies better than either. This will be found true, however "good government" is defined. The traditional reactionary argument has been that majority rule is tyranny while monarchy and oligarchy are good; and the traditional radical argument has been that monarchy and oligarchy are tyrannies while democracy is good. Both arguments are equally inconsistent and equally confused. Neither argues the other's point. The question is not which is the better government but which is more likely to allow a free government. Majority rule, if conceived in the terms in which it is usually defined today, is incompatible with freedom. But it is also true that monarchy or oligarchy are just as tyrannical if the monarch or the ruling minority base their rule on a claim to be right or more nearly right than the rest. If perfection is claimed for the ruler, there is no difference in the effects on freedom between one-man rule, the rule of the few, or the rule of the many. What is incompatible with freedom is not the number of sovereigns but the claim to perfection. Majority rule is neither a greater nor a lesser danger to freedom than one-man rule or oligarchy.

Good government cannot be planned; it cannot be ensured by legal or institutional means. For good government is a function of those incalculable and intangible factors: the moral character of a society, and the genius of the individual statesman. Monarchy and oligarchy are intrinsically neither better nor worse than democracy. It is impossible even to establish as a hypothesis which of these will more often be likely to be good than the others. There is no answer to the Aristotelian question. Indeed, there is no question if we believe that man is imperfect though responsible. For the Aristotelian question in itself denies freedom. And the assumption of freedom denies the possibility of any "best government."

There can be no freedom if the majority is deemed perfect and unlimited. But the very imperfection and limitation of man and of government can be better expressed on a democratic than on any other basis.

In the first place, the need for majority approval is one of the most stringent and most potent limitations on government ever devised. Though not enough in itself, the need to obtain the consent of the governed is a powerful restriction of governmental power and a safeguard of political freedom. Nothing is less in concordance with the idea of freedom than a government that is just a slave of the majority. But no government is more likely to be a free government than one limited by the consent of the governed as expressed in a majority decision.

Far more important even is the use of popular assemblies, of popular vote and elections as an instrument for the realization of that most important requirement of a free government: self-government. No government can be free in which the citizens do not participate in the responsibilities and decisions. The majority vote can be made the most satisfactory device known to political experience for the realization of the greatest possible approximation to the ideal of self-government. But it should never be forgotten that it can be used just as well to deprive the individual citizen of his responsibility.

Popular government may be made more nearly a free government than either monarchy or oligarchy. Majority consent may provide a limitation of government. And the mechanism of votes and elections may be used to realize self-government. But popular government degenerates into tyranny if it becomes government of the divine right of a perfect or near-perfect majority. It dissolves in anarchy if it is abused as the means through which the citizen shirks his responsibility and evades his duty to participate in the social and political decisions.

This theory of a free popular government will not surprise anyone who is even superficially acquainted with the history of political theory. It is substantially the theory of Christian freedom which underlay the first great democratic development in Europe: that of the fourteenth and fifteenth centuries. The political theorists of that time understood perfectly the need for political freedom, the function of popular government and the danger of majority rule. This theory of popular government was also that of the Glorious Revolution of 1688, of the *Federalist,* of Burke and of all the other "liberal Conservatives" down to Lord Acton and Mr. Justice Holmes. What has changed in the course of the last five centuries is the concrete, institutional realization; the basic theory has remained the same.

Yet there is a fundamental difference between the traditional Christian theory of freedom and the solution of the late eighteenth century on which was based the nineteenth-century free society. The original theory was concerned only with formal political freedom; it was a theory of "free government," not one of a "free society." The Founding Fathers in America, however, and Burke in England centered their efforts on the establishment of a free society. They successfully achieved an integration of free government and free society.

They not only understood that a free government is not in itself a free society. They also saw that without an integration of the two there could be no real safeguard against the twin dangers to free government: the degeneration of majority consent into majority rule, and the degeneration of popular self-government into party tyranny.

The great innovation of the late eighteenth century "liberal conservatives" was the juxtaposition of political government and social rule. The nineteenth century based political power consciously on a principle of legitimacy different from that on which social rule was based. It organized government and society in different institutions. And it limited the rule in the one sphere by that in the other. It is perfectly true, as has often been said by critics of the nineteenth-century solution, that there is no natural separation of political government and society. It is a purely artificial one, made by man in order to make possible a free government and a free society. It is also true that it cannot be demanded that there be no government in society. The socially constitutive sphere—whatever it is—is far too important and far too "political" to go without government. But as already explained, the separation of the two spheres never had the meaning of "laissez faire" which nineteenth-century liberalism read into it. Far from demanding that there be no rule in the socially constitutive sphere, the solution of the late eighteenth century provided for a definite organization of power in that sphere. It demanded only that this government of society be different from the political government proper in its institutions and in the basis of its legitimacy.

To the great political thinkers of the generation of 1776 we owe whatever freedom there has been in the Western world since. Their starting point was the idea that the consent of the majority as the ethical basis of free government had to be counterbalanced. Politically, legally, and institutionally there has to be a competing ethical principle for the power in the socially constitutive sphere. And this principle in the socially constitutive sphere had to be limited by a competing principle in political government. The starting point of Madison, Jefferson, Burke, and Hamilton was the conviction that *any one ethical principle of power will become an absolutist, i.e., a tyrannical, principle unless checked, controlled, and limited by a competing principle.* Constitutional safeguards on which the past has always relied are not good enough. They have always been overthrown. A monist basis of power must become an absolutist one. Because it is exclusive, it must come to be accepted as perfect—and as soon as this happens freedom is impossible.

As a philosophical principle, the separation of government in the political sphere from social rule was not new. It is as old as the Christian theory of free government. It was St. Augustine who first separated society: the City of God, from temporal government. The same thought was expressed in the famous theory of the "two swords": the temporal one of political government wielded by the emperor, the spiritual one of social order wielded by the Church, through which the High Middle Ages attempted to find a free society. It was brought out in very clear form in Chief Justice Coke's juxtaposition of the common law against the law of King and Parlia-

ment during the reign of the Stuarts, which later became so decisive as the theoretical basis for that great
bulwark of freedom, the United States Supreme Court,
with its right of judicial review of Congressional Acts.
The refusal of the West to adopt a unitarian social order
may even be said to have been the real issue in the break
with the Byzantine Empire in which government and
society had become fused in the person of the emperor.
Altogether the basic idea is as old as His counsel to ren-
der unto Caesar what is Caesar's, and unto the Lord
what is the Lord's.

As a working principle of practical politics, however,
the separation of government and society originated
with the generation of 1776 and 1787—the Founding
Fathers of the American Revolution and the liberal conservatives such as Burke in England. They were the first
who clearly recognized it to be the basis of freedom.
They also understood that the essence of the solution
is the separation of the two spheres and the juxtaposition
of two independent principles of legitimate power. In
all earlier theories the philosophical juxtaposition of
the two spheres had led to an attempt in practical politics to subordinate the one to the other. In the solution
of 1776 for the first time they were used to balance
each other.

In the nineteenth-century society both spheres were
autonomous, equal, and legitimate. In both the basis

was the responsible decision, the responsible participation of the citizens. But the basis of this rule was a different one in each sphere: majority consent made government legitimate; private property ruled society. For the economic sphere was the socially constitutive sphere of the nineteenth century. Property rights always limited majority rights and prevented their degeneration into majority rule. Majority rights always checked property rights and prevented their degeneration into plutocracy.

That property rights were the basis for social rule in the particular society of the nineteenth century is not so important for the general principle. What matters is that a free society and a free government are possible only if there are not one but two competing bases of power: one of social and one of political organization. The great and lasting contribution of the generation of 1776 to the theory and practice of freedom is the realization that a free popular government—however correct theoretically—cannot be prevented in practice from degenerating into mob tyranny or into the despotism of the demagogue, unless there is a dualistic basis of power. Freedom will endure only if the free government in the political sphere and the free rule in the socially constitutive sphere balance and check each other. This discovery represented the greatest advance in political thinking since the days of the early Christian humanism of the

City Republics of 1350 or 1400. It also was the first fully satisfactory answer to the old question: how is the realization of a free society actually possible? It must therefore be the starting point for all concrete political thinking about the free society of the future.

CHAPTER SEVEN

FROM ROUSSEAU TO HITLER

IT is almost an axiom in contemporary political and historical literature that our freedom has its roots in the Enlightenment and the French Revolution. So general is this belief, so complete its acceptance, that the descendants of the eighteenth-century rationalists have pre-empted for themselves the very name of Liberty in their designation as Liberals.

It cannot be denied that the Enlightenment and the French Revolution contributed to the freedom of the nineteenth century. But their contribution was entirely negative; they were the dynamite that blew away the debris of the old structure. In no way, however, did they contribute to the foundation of the new structure of freedom on which the nineteenth-century order was built. On the contrary: The Enlightenment, the French Revolution, and their successors down to the rationalist Liberalism of our days are in irreconcilable opposition to freedom. Fundamentally, rationalist Liberalism is totalitarian.

And every totalitarian movement during the last two

hundred years of Western history has grown out of the Liberalism of its time. There is a straight line from Rousseau to Hitler—a line that takes in Robespierre, Marx, and Stalin. All of them grew out of the failure of the rationalist Liberalism of their times. They all retained the essence of their respective liberal creeds, and all used the same mechanism to convert the latent and ineffective totalitarianism of the rationalist into the open and effective totalitarianism of the revolutionary despot. Far from being the roots of freedom, the Enlightenment and the French Revolution were the seeds of the totalitarian despotism which threatens the world today. The fathers and grandfathers of Hitlerism are not medieval feudalism or nineteenth-century romanticism but Bentham and Condorcet, the orthodox economists, and the liberal constitutionalists, Darwin, Freud, and the Behaviorists.

The great discovery of the Enlightenment was that human reason is absolute. On this discovery were based not only all subsequent liberal creeds but also all subsequent totalitarian creeds from Rousseau on. It was no accident that Robespierre installed a Goddess of Reason; his symbolism was cruder than that of the later revolutionaries but not really very different. Nor was it an accident that the French Revolution chose a living person to act the role of Goddess of Reason. The whole point of the rationalist philosophy is that it attributes to actual living men the perfection of absolute reason. The symbols and slogans have changed. Where the "scientific philosopher" was supreme in 1750, it was the sociologist with his economic utilitarianism and the "pleasure-pain calculus" a hundred years later. Today it is the "scientific psycho-biologist" with his determinism of race and propaganda. But we fight today basically the same totalitarian absolutism that first was formulated by the Enlighteners and Encyclopedists— the rationalists of 1750—and that first led to a revolutionary tyranny in the Terror of 1793.

It must be understood that not everything that is called liberalism is of necessity an absolutist creed. Every liberal movement, it is true, contains the seeds of a totalitarian philosophy—just as every conservative movement contains a tendency to become reactionary. On the Continent of Europe there never were any liberal movements or parties which were not totalitarian in their fundamental beliefs. In the United States the totalitarian element was strongly represented from the start—based as much upon the influence from Europe as upon the Puritan tradition. And since the last war liberalism everywhere has become absolutist. Today it is true, almost without reservation, that the liberal is an absolutist in his objective creed.

But for a hundred years before 1914 Great Britain had a liberal movement that was not absolutist, not incompatible with freedom and not based upon a man-made absolute reason. The United States had during the same period a liberal tradition which was as much opposed to absolutist liberalism as it was close to English liberalism. This free and antitotalitarian tradition, which was expressed in its most lucid form by Mr. Justice Holmes, was usually not the dominant liberal tradition in America. It was often completely overshadowed by the absolutist liberalism of which the Abolitionists and the radical Republicans of the Reconstruction Period are the outstanding representatives. It produced, however, in Lincoln the nineteenth century's greatest symbol of an anti-absolutist and truly liberal liberalism. It became politically effective in Populism—the most indigenous American political movement since the early days of the republic. And the New Deal, though very largely dominated by rationalism, owed its appeal and political effectiveness to its populist heritage.

The fundamental difference between the free and constructive Anglo-American liberalism of the nineteenth century, and the absolutist and destructive liberalism of the Enlightenment and of our Liberals today, is that the first is based on religion and Christianity, while the second is rationalist. The true liberalism grew out of a religious renunciation of rationalism. The English Liberal party of the nineteenth century was based partly on the tradition of the settlement of 1688. But the main element was the "Nonconformist Conscience." The first was a reaffirmation of freedom against the rationalist absolutism of both, Cromwellian theocracy and centralized monarchy. The second sprang from the great religious revivals of the eighteenth century, notably Wesley's Methodism and Low Church Evangelism. Both were appeals to Christian love, faith, and humility. And both were directed against the rationalism of their time —Methodism against the Enlightenment, the Evangelical movement against the utilitarianism of Bentham and the classical economists.

In the United States similarly the true and genuinely "liberal" liberalism traces back to a religious protest against rationalist absolutism. Its forefather, Roger Williams, attacked in the name of Christian freedom the rationalist theocracy of the New England divines who had set up their scripture-learning as absolute reason. And the Populist movement—whatever its economic causes—rested squarely upon an evangelical protest against rationalist utilitarianism and orthodox economists. It was an invocation of the dignity of man against the tyranny of absolute reason and of "inevitable economic progress."

Even this free liberalism is of only limited effectiveness politically. It cannot overcome a revolution. It cannot develop the institutions of social or political life. For even at its best it is primarily a protest against institutions. Its first function is the defense of the individual against authority; its basis is an appeal to the brotherhood of man beyond politics and society, beyond government and social function and status. The true liberalism can therefore be effective only after a functioning society has come into being. But within these limitations it is both constructive and effective.

Today, however, there is no such truly "liberal" liberalism anywhere—except in some scattered remnants in the United States and England. What we know today as "liberalism" is exclusively rationalist. But the rationalist is not only basically totalitarian. He is also unconstructive. He must fail in politics; and in his failure he threatens freedom, because his failure is the chance for the revolutionary totalitarian.

2.

That objectively the rationalist's creed is incompatible with freedom is no denial of the individual rationalist's or liberal's good will or good faith. Doubtless the individual rationalist liberal believes sincerely that he, and he alone, stands for freedom and against tyranny. There is also no doubt that he subjectively abhors totalitarian tyranny and all it represents. And in turn, he is the first victim of the despots.

But these antitotalitarian sentiments of the individual

rationalist are entirely ineffective in politics. Altogether rationalism is incapable of positive political action. It can function only in opposition. It can never make the step from negative critique to constructive policy. And it always opposes the free institutions of society fully as much as the unfree and oppressive ones.

The rationalist liberal sees his function in the opposition to the injustices, superstitions and prejudices of his time. But this opposition to injustice is only a part of a general hostility to all institutions of society including free and just ones. The Enlighteners, for instance, swept away aristocratic privileges, serfdom and religious intolerance. They also destroyed provincial autonomies and local self-government; and no country on the Continent of Europe has ever fully recovered from this blow to freedom. They attacked clerical abuses, privileges, and oppression. They also degraded the churches of Europe into administrative arms of the political government. They did their best to deprive religious life of its social autonomy and moral authority. And the full force of Enlightened scorn was directed against independent courts and against the common law. The insistence of the eighteenth-century rationalist on a "rationally perfect" law code and on state-controlled courts leads straight to the omnipotent total state. It is no accident that the "free" Anglo-American liberalism of the nineteenth century was based to a large extent on these very institutions which the Enlighteners had repudiated: local self-government, free autonomous churches, the common law, and an independent judiciary.

The rationalist not only destroys and opposes existing institutions without principle of selection; he is completely incapable of developing new institutions for the old ones which he destroys. He does not even see the need for constructive activity. For to him the good is only the absence of evil. He thinks that he has done his job if he has criticized away bad or oppressive institutions. But in political and social life nothing is effective unless it is given institutional realization. Society must be organized on the basis of functional power-relations. To subvert is only legitimate in politics if it leads to the construction of something better. But just to sweep away something—however bad—is no solution. And unless a functioning institution is put into the place of the destroyed institution, the ensuing collapse of social life will breed evils which may be even worse than the one that was originally destroyed.

The inability of the rationalist to construct and the consequences of his political impotence show most tellingly in the Old South, not only because the evil attacked and destroyed was slavery, that greatest of all social evils, but because the failure to give the South a new society for the old it had lost was most spectacular. And the inability of the rationalists to integrate into society the Jew whose ghetto community they had dissolved is one important cause of modern anti-Semitism.

Wherever the rationalist liberal has come to power, he always failed. The fate of Kerenski's Liberal government in Russia, which collapsed into Bolshevism after half a year of political paralysis, is only the most obvious case. The German Social Democrats were equally incapable of political action when they came to power in 1918. They had been an extremely useful opposition under the Kaiser. There is no doubt that their leaders were sincere and honorable, that they were capable administrators, personally courageous and popular. Yet what is amazing is not that they failed but that they lasted as long as they did. For by 1922 or 1923 they had become completely bankrupt. The same is true of French Radicals, of Italian Liberals, or of Spanish Democrats. And the "reformer" in the United States also normally ended in frustration. The history of every city government in America shows the political ineffectiveness of these well-meaning rationalists.

It is impossible to explain so extraordinary and consistent a record of failure as one of circumstances and accidents. The real reason is that rationalist liberalism is by its very nature condemned to political sterility. It lives in constant conflict with itself. It is based on two principles which exclude each other. It can only deny but it cannot act.

On the one hand the rationalist believes in an absolute reason. Yesterday it was inevitable progress or national harmony between individual self-interest and the common weal. Today it is the creed that libido, frustration, and glands explain all personal or group conflicts. On the other hand, rationalist liberalism believes that its absolutes are the result of rational deduction, are provable and rationally incontrovertible. It is the essence of rationalist liberalism that it proclaims its absolutes to be rationally evident.

Absolute reason can, however, never be rational; it can never be proved or disproved by logic. Absolute reason is by its very nature above and before rational argument. Logical deduction can and must be based upon an absolute reason but can never prove it. If truly religious, an absolute principle is superrational—a true metaphysical principle which gives a valid basis of rational logic. If man-made and man-proclaimed, absolute reason must be irrational and in insoluble conflict with rational logic and rational means.

All the basic dogmas of rationalism during the last hundred and fifty years were not only irrational but basically antirational. This was true of the philosophical rationalism of the Enlighteners who proclaimed the inherent reasonableness of man. It was true of the utilitarian rationalism of the generation of 1848 which saw in the individual's greed the mechanism through which the "invisible hand" of nature promoted the common good. It is particularly true of the twentieth-century rationalism which sees man as psychologically and biologically determined. Every one of these principles denies not only free will. It denies human reason. And every one of these principles can be translated into political action only by force and by an absolute ruler.

But this the rationalist cannot admit. He must maintain that his principles are rational and that they can be made effective by rational means. He maintains as a dogma that his principles are rationally evident. Hence the rationalist liberal cannot attempt to translate them into political action expect through rational conversion —which attempt must fail. On the one hand he cannot respect any opposition, for it can only be opposition to absolute truth. On the other hand, he cannot fight it. For error—and all opposition to his absolute truth must be error to a rationalist—can only be due to lack of information. Nothing shows this better than the saying current during the twenties and early thirties in Europe as well as in the United States that an *intelligent* person must be on the Left. And today the belief in the omnipotence of propaganda expresses openly and clearly the absolutist basis and the self-contradiction of the rationalist creed.

On the one hand, the rationalist liberal cannot compromise. His is a perfectionist creed which allows of no concession. Anyone who refuses to see the light is an unmitigated blackguard with whom political relations are impossible. On the other hand, the rationalist cannot fight or suppress enemies. He cannot admit their existence. There can be only misjudged or misinformed people who, of necessity, will see reason when the incontrovertible evidence of the rational truth is presented to them. The rationalist liberal is caught between holy wrath at conspirators and educational zeal for the misinformed. He always knows what is right, necessary, and good—and it always is simple and easy. But he can never do it. For he can neither compromise for power nor fight for it. He is always paralyzed politically: ultra-bold in theory and timid in action, strong in opposition and helpless in power, right on paper but incapable in politics.

3.

It is the tragedy of the rationalist liberal that there is only one way from his position to political effectiveness: totalitarianism. His subjectively sincere belief in freedom can objectively lead only to tyranny. For there is only one way out of the political sterility of the rationalist liberal: to drop the rationalism and to become openly totalitarian, absolutist and revolutionary.

During the Enlightenment it was Rousseau who made the fatal step from rationalism and pretended rationality to openly irrational and antirational totalitarianism. There is no pretense that the "general will" is rationally ascertainable or rationally realizable. It is admittedly an irrational absolute which defies rational analysis and which is outside and beyond rational comprehension. It exists—but how, where and why no one knows. It must prevail—naturally, since it is perfect and absolute. Whoever is in possession of reason, whoever understands the supreme will of society, is entitled and, indeed, is duty bound to enforce it upon majority, minority and individual alike. Freedom lies only in the perfect realization of the *volonté générale*. There is no pretense in Rousseau of individual reason or individual freedom.

It is true that Rousseau insisted upon the small unit of the city-state with its direct, nonrepresentative democracy as the only perfect form of government. And he laid down an inalienable right of the individual to disagree by leaving his society. This has been taken as an indication of his desire for individual freedom. But in a world in which these conditions were as impossible of fulfillment as in that of the middle eighteenth century, they can hardly be taken as anything but romantic flourishes in an otherwise unyieldingly realistic and unromantic totalitarianism. Otherwise Hitler's "offer" of emigration to the Jews would also be "freedom."

Rousseau's plunge into the irrational absolute made the basic concepts of the Enlightenment politically effective. Rousseau was right when he saw in the repudiation of rationalism the basic difference of his system from that of the *philosophes*. His open irrationalism enabled him to shake off the fetters which had condemned the Encyclopedists to political ineffectiveness. Where they believed in the slow and painstaking rational process of education and scientific investigation, he believed in the inner light of revelation. They tried to define man as within the laws of physics. But Rousseau saw man as a political being acting upon impulse and emotion. Where they saw the gradual rationalist improvement, he believed in the millennium that could and would be established by that most irrational of forces: the revolution. No doubt he knew more about politics and society than all the Enlighteners taken together. His view of man in society was realistic where the rationalist Enlighteners had been hopelessly and pathetically romantic.

In fact, Rousseau can be fought only if his basis is attacked: the belief in a man-made absolute reason, the belief that he himself possessed it and that whoever has absolute reason has the right and the duty to enforce it.

Because Rousseau threw overboard the rationalism

of the Enlightenment, he became the great political force he has been to our day. Because he retained the Enlighteners' belief in human perfectibility, he denied human freedom and became the great totalitarian and revolutionary who lit the fuse for a universal blaze equalled only by our generation.

Rousseau's method has been followed every time a politically sterile, because rationalist, liberalism was converted into a politically effective nonrationalist totalitarianism. The first to follow in his footsteps was Karl Marx. Just as Rousseau appeared when the Enlighteners of the early eighteenth century had shown their political ineffectiveness, so Marx began when the utilitarian rationalists of the early nineteenth century had foundered politically. In 1848 rationalist liberalism was bankrupt. It had had power thrust into its lap through the breakdown of reactionary monarchy in France, Austria, Germany and Spain; and, without exception, it proved completely incapable of doing anything with it except lose it again.

Marx converted the impotent rationalist liberalism of his time into a politically potent force by dropping its rationalism and adopting an openly irrational absolutism. He kept the absolute of the contemporary liberals, the thesis of economic determination which sees man as rational Economic Man. But he eliminated the

rationalism which expected the attainment of the perfect economic society from the free and rational economic action of the individual. Instead he proclaimed an
irrational principle: that of the determination of human
action by the class situation of the individual. This principle denies man's capacity for rational action, thinking,
and analysis. Everybody's deeds and thoughts are the
result of a class situation which is beyond the individual's control and understanding. Marx kept the utilitarian's historical materialism; but for the materialism of
inevitable harmony he substituted that of the equally
inevitable class struggle. He kept the rationalist belief
in the essential perfection of man. But he confined perfection to the one proletarian class.

Marx went one step further than Rousseau. To Rousseau the revolution was necessary as it must indeed be
to every totalitarian. But it was not inevitable. Rousseau
left an element of doubt; Marx left none. In a truly
apocalyptic vision he saw the inevitability of the revolution which would usher in the millennium. Rationally,
the Marxist belief that the future will inevitably belong
to the perfect classless society *because* all the past has
been one of class-societies is blatant, arrant, and mysti-
cal nonsense. Politically, the very antirationality of this
article of faith was its strength. It not only gave belief;
it also made possible the mastermind, the revolutionary
philosopher-tyrant who, schooled in the dialectics of the

inevitable, could claim absolute knowledge at every time.

It is politically very unimportant that Marx claimed to be "scientific"—just as it is unimportant that Machiavelli was a member of the Roman Catholic Church in good standing. Marx would still have had the same political appeal if he had never written one line of *Das Kapital*. He was effective not because he is the most brilliant historian of capitalist development, nor because he is the most boring, pedantic, and inconsistent theoretician of capitalist economics. He took a world and a society which was already convinced of an absolutist thesis regarding the nature of man, and he made it possible for this thesis to become politically effective.

Rousseau became a tremendous political force because the revolution did happen. Marx—though much inferior to Rousseau as a politician, a psychologist, and a philosopher—became a force of equal strength even though the revolution did not happen; it was sufficient that, unlike Rousseau's, Marx's revolution was inevitable.

Marxism still has its revolutionary appeal in basically preindustrial countries: in Mexico, Spain, or in raw-material producing colonies. That the Marxist revolution occurred in Russia, the least industrialized country of Europe, was no accident. For only in an early industrial or preindustrial society does Marxism make sense. Only in its very first stages does the industrial system exhibit the split of society into a handful of monopolistic entrepreneurs on the one side and an amorphous, dispossessed, proletarian mass on the other, which Marx had proclaimed as inevitable. As soon as industrialization proceeds beyond the initial stage, it develops an employed, yet professional, middle class of engineers, salesmen, chemists, accountants, and so forth. This class not only refutes all Marxist assumptions and repudiates the entire Marxist creed. It becomes the functionally most important class in the industrial system. Wherever this class has been developed to any extent, Marxism ceases to be an effective political force.

In the Western countries Marxism could have come to power only in Marx's own time; that is, while these countries were still in a very early stage of industrial development. Marx himself expressed this in his prophecy that his revolution would come before 1900. That it failed to come was due to two antitotalitarian forces which Marx did not see. There was first the strong antitotalitarian tradition of England. The heritage of the successful conservative counterrevolution against Enlightenment and French Revolution was still alive and vigorous in Victorian England. Both Conservatives and Liberals based themselves on it. England repudiated Marxism because of its totalitarianism. And though the conservative tradition was absent on the Continent, England's prestige as the social and political leader was so great as to prevent the victory of a creed which England ignored. The second and even more effective anti-totalitarian force in the second half of the nineteenth century was America. Her free society, her free immigration, her free land, her equal opportunities acted— physically and spiritually—as the safety valve of European society which prevented an explosion. It was above all the Civil War which restored Europe's faith in freedom after the severe shock of 1848.

But while Marxism failed as a revolutionary creed in the industrial countries, it made a lasting impact on political beliefs on the Continent of Europe. It prepared the great masses for totalitarianism. It made them ready to accept the logic of man-made, absolutist, apocalyptic visions. For this alone Marxism deserves to be called the father of Hitlerism. It also bequeathed to the totalitarianism of our time the mold and the structure of ideas and political thought. What Marx did with the broken-down rationalist liberalism of his time—the liberalism of the classical economists and of the utilitarians—Hitler has been doing with the broken-down rationalism of our time—that of the natural scientists and psychologists.

Mr. Jacques Barzun of Columbia University has shown in a book of brilliant insight, *Marx, Darwin and*

Wagner how the *economic* determinism of the early nineteenth-century absolutists had become *biological* determinism by the end of the century. What he has not shown—as, indeed, lies outside the field he has staked out for himself—is the development of biological determinism into a rationalist creed and its supplementation by a psychological determinism. The roots of Nazism lie in the biological determinism which began with Darwin. And the meaning and the political structure of Hitlerism can be understood only in the light of the philosophical and political development of this new— and so far last—set of man-made absolutes.

It is not the theory of evolution or the theory of neuroses which interests us in this connection. It is rather the philosophy developed from them which expresses itself in such popular sayings as "Man is what his glands make him," or "Man is what his childhood frustrations make him." No doubt, both sayings are literally true. They are just as true as the statements that man is what his economic interests, education, digestion, social status, religion, or physical strength and conformation make him. Every single one of these statements is incontrovertible; yet any one by itself is meaningless. But in the sixty years between the *Origin of the Species* and the Great War of 1914-18 the explanation of man as biological-psychological man was gradually adopted as the basis of European rationalist liberalism.

The Eugenists on the one hand, the Behaviorists on the other—to mention only the extremists—developed the claim that man is perfectible, either biologically or psychologically.

By 1900 the belief in psycho-biological determinism had begun to be popular and was replacing the worn-out economic determinism. The great popularizer of the new creed was G. B. Shaw. *Candida* anticipates all of Adler and Jung; *Back to Methuselah,* a good deal of Hitler. In the political and social sphere the change became perceptible at about the same time—in the fear of the "Yellow Peril"; in the flare-up of anti-Semitism in France, Austria and Russia; in the development of advertising, public-relations men, and propaganda newspapers.

Where the Enlighteners had tried to educate, where the utilitarians had tried to establish free trade and a stock exchange, the new rationalists tried to organize on a racial or "folk" basis and to manage by propaganda and other methods of modern psychology. Like their predecessor rationalists, they had an absolute concept of the nature of man. They saw him as a creature of genes, chromosomes, and glands; and as formed and molded by measurable psychological experiences. Hence they also believed in human perfection, or at least perfectibility. They proclaimed the absolute reason of those who understand and master human breeding

and human psychological analysis. All those irrationals
—more irrational perhaps and certainly more antirational than any of the preceding man-made absolutes
since the Enlightenment—were held to be "scientifi-
cally" proven, attainable by rational means, and therefore "objective truth."

The first World War shattered this new rationalism
even before it had had time to develop into a fully-
fledged political force. The War could not be comprised
or understood by means of the "rationality" of the
psycho-biologist or, indeed, by any liberal rationalism.
The War was real, most real, as was the postwar decade
following it. In this crisis of the new rationalism, Nazism made the decisive step toward a full and politically
effective totalitarianism which could explain the realities. It took both the biological determinism and the
psychological explanation of man and set them up as
irrational absolutes. At the same time it proclaimed
those who understood "race" and "propaganda" to be
perfect and to be entitled to absolute, uncontestable
political leadership and control.

The one great difference between Hitler's conversion
of rationalist liberalism into totalitarianism and the
work of his predecessors, Rousseau and Marx, lies in
the open elevation of the one Master over organized society. It is, of course, true that the great mass of individ-

uals are deindividualized in Nazism to the point where their identity is lost; but that was also true of Rousseauan or Marxist totalitarianism. But in Hitler's system one man is elevated above all his fellow men and above all society: the Leader. Actually, such an individual despot was inevitable in the theories of both Rousseau and Marx, as the developments of the French and Russian revolutions clearly showed. But only the Nazi revolution admitted this. The Nazis made the necessity of the perfect leader into a political asset of the first magnitude. Whereas Rousseau had only preached the revolution and Marx had predicted it, the leadership principle enabled Hitler to make it. Politically, his totalitarianism is the most effective and the deadliest one. It is the one in which the philosophical and political conclusions from the absolutist assumption of human perfection and perfectibility are drawn most extensively and most rigorously.

The basis for Hitlerism—as for the preceding totalitarianisms—had been supplied ready-made by the rationalist liberals. The method had been used twice before with great success. What Hitler added was a moral cynicism which would have been impossible in the times of Marx and Rousseau but which proved possible and even popular at a time when psychology had taught that there is no moral core in man. For the explosive force of Nazism which the Fuehrer Prinzip supplied, Hitler has to thank the psychoanalysts and personality psychologists.

To sum up: When the Enlightenment was threatened with collapse, Rousseau replaced its rationally attainable perfection with the irrational and even mystic "general will." When the post-Napoleonic rationalist liberalism of the utilitarians, and orthodox economists had collapsed in the abortive revolutions of 1848, Marx replaced their rationalist absolutes with the irrational perfection of the proletariat and the inevitability of the classless society. And when the rationalist psycho-biological determinism of modern science, of Darwin, Freud and the Behaviorists collapsed under the impact of World War and depression, Hitler proclaimed the principles of the biologists and psychologists in the irrationalism of race and propaganda.

None of the totalitarians changed the basis. Rousseau kept all the beliefs of the Enlightenment regarding the nature of man and society. Marx took from the orthodox economists the assertion that man is basically an economic animal. Hitler asserts with the biologists and psychologists that man is basically glands, heredity, and nervous impressions. None of the revolutionaries had to add anything to the fundamental beliefs of the rationalism of their days. All they had to do was to change the absolute truth and reason from a rationalist into an irrationalist pseudoreligious principle.

Rousseau proclaimed that the "general will" would assert itself precisely because it could not be rationally ascertained. Marx promised that the future would belong to the classless society precisely because all the past had been a history of class war. Hitler claims the millennium for the pure Nordic race precisely because the past had been dominated by the "mongrel races." To these irrational absolutes totalitarianism owes its appeal to a people disillusioned by rationalism. To them it owes its revolutionary force and the fanaticism which it inspires. And to them it also owes its absolute denial of all freedom and the inevitable emergence of a dictator who claims perfection.

It follows from this analysis that the rationalist liberal cannot fight totalitarianism effectively. He is always in the position of that first great rationalist liberal: Socrates. Like that greatest and wisest of pre-Christian thinkers he believes that the good can be ascertained infallibly by man. Like Socrates he also believes that it can be taught rationally and that to understand the good is to be good. In other words, the rationalist liberal always knows what is good; he sets up an absolute against which there can be no opposition. By denying the possibility of evil—for man can err only through lack of information, but he can never sin—he denies responsibility without which there can be no meaningful choice, that is, no freedom. But, like Socrates, he can never translate this belief into political action since he believes his absolutism to be rational. He assumes that it is effective by its mere existence without any organization of power or any realization in institutions. On the liberal basis the one and only thing that is possible is a critique of the past.

Totalitarianism comes when liberalism has failed. And it comes as a direct result of this failure. There is no doubt that the individual rationalist hates the totalitarianism of his time deeply and sincerely; no doubt that he wants to fight it. But he cannot really attack it. For the totalitarians do only what the rationalists should have done on the basis of their philosophical beliefs. If Socrates really believed the oracle that he was the wisest man in all Greece—and he certainly acted on the assumption that he was the only wise man in Greece—he would have had the moral duty to set himself up as a tyrant. He could not do it because he believed his wisdom to be rational and to be effective without political means. Thereby he not only resigned himself to political impotence; he also paved the way for the real totalitarians. The Thirty Tyrants accepted the Socratian basis without the Socratian rationalism. They were thus able to proclaim that everything they did was good because they themselves were good.

It is certain that Socrates would have bitterly disapproved of them. It is at least highly probable that the Thirty Tyrants would have been forced to kill him had he not been killed earlier by the alliance of traditionalist reactionaries and relativist anarchists, which is so typical for the eve of a revolution. Yet, in spite of his subjective opposition to the totalitarian tyrants, Socrates would have been entirely powerless against them. They executed politically only what he had taught philosophically: the supremacy of those who had attained wisdom. However wrong the accusations against Socrates, the masses were right on one point: he fathered the totalitarian would-be tyrants precisely because he was a rationalist liberal.

Translated into present-day terms, this means that we cannot expect any effective political or philosophical resistance against the fascist totalitarianism of our days from the rationalist liberal. There is no question that the English, German, or French socialist or the American radical is sincerely and honestly opposed to Hitlerism; his personal integrity is not at all in doubt. Nor does it mean that he will not be very effective as a soldier, for in the trenches it is his individual conviction alone that counts. The conclusion from our analysis is only that rational liberalism, however sincerely opposed to totalitarian fascism, cannot be expected to evolve a free alternative to totalitarian slavery. It cannot offer a solution for a free industrial society; it cannot overcome totalitarianism as a principle even though it may defeat the totalitarian dictators in the field.

It is significant that in the United States the liberals of yesterday—the semi-socialist planners—have come to be known as the "totalitarian liberals." Their only answer to Hitler's belief that propaganda determines the beliefs of the individual is to substitute "good propaganda"—that is, their own propaganda—for Hitler's "bad propaganda." But the rationalist liberal cannot admit that the conviction that propaganda creates and determines ideas, loyalties, and beliefs is in itself a denial of freedom. He refuses to see that the pseudo religion of propaganda conceives of man as determined by, and enslaved to, the dulcet voice of the radio. And he fails to understand that it does not really matter whether propaganda is "good" or "bad" as long as it is assumed that propaganda makes the man. For the rationalist liberal shares Hitler's conviction that man is psychologically determined.

The revolutionary totalitarianism of today cannot be overcome either by the revolutionary totalitarianism of yesterday—Marxism—or by the totalitarianism of the rationalist liberals with their belief in biological, psychological, or economic determinism. Actually, both the

Marxist and the rationalist liberal add to the strength of the revolutionary totalitarianism, however sincerely they oppose it. Their opposition is politically completely ineffective. But their latent absolutism makes the masses ready for the politically effective absolutism of the revolutionary totalitarian.

CHAPTER EIGHT

THE CONSERVATIVE COUNTER-
REVOLUTION OF 1776

JUST as popular and just as fallacious as the belief that the Enlightenment fathered nineteenth-century freedom is the belief that the American Revolution was based on the same principles as the French Revolution, and that it was actually its forerunner. Every history book in the United States or in Europe says so; and not a few of the chief actors both in the American and French Revolutions shared the belief. Yet it is a complete distortion of all facts.

The American Revolution was based on principles completely contrary to those of the Enlightenment and the French Revolution. In intention and effect it was a successful countermovement against the very rationalist despotism of the Enlightenment which provided the political foundation for the French Revolution. Though the French Revolution happened later in time, it had politically and philosophically been anticipated by the American Revolution. The conservatives of 1776 and 1787 fought and overcame the spirit of the French

Revolution so that the American development actually represents a more advanced stage in history than the *Etats Généraux,* the Terror, and Napoleon. Far from being a revolt against the old tyranny of feudalism, the American Revolution was a conservative counterrevolution in the name of freedom against the new tyranny of rationalist liberalism and Enlightened Despotism.

The liberal totalitarianism of the Enlightenment and the revolutionary totalitarianism of the French Revolution could only destroy the *ancien régime.* At best they might have been able to put in the place of the old, hopelessly collapsed, premercantile society a functioning but despotic mercantile society. Even that is most doubtful as Robespierre's Permanent Revolution or Napoleon's Permanent War were hardly more successful as a basis of a functioning society than Hitler's creed. But the American Revolution succeeded in building not only a functioning, but a free, society.

Even after their defeat by the forces of the conservative American counterrevolution, the principles of the French Revolution—the ideas of 1789—have continued to make for tyranny. They have provided the modes of thought and mentality for every subsequent totalitarian philosophy. The freedom of the Western world during the nineteenth century and up to this day has been based upon the ideas, principles, and institutions of the American conservative counterrevolution of 1776.

The common fallacy regarding the nature and effects of the American Revolution has been greatly aided by the conventional departmentalization of historical writing which has erected almost watertight bulkheads between American and European history. The American Revolution is thus treated as an event of exclusive or primary American importance. Its motives, issues, and effects are seen as confined to the American Continent. The function and place of the Revolution of 1776 and of the Constitution of 1787 in the general development of the Western world have hardly received serious attention. This is a falsification not only of European history but of American history too.

Actually, the American Revolution was as much a European as an American event. It may even be said to have been more important as a European than as an American development—if the importance of historical events is to be measured by the extent to which they introduce new and unexpected factors. The Thirteen Colonies would sooner or later have become independent as one nation in the normal course of events. The best minds in England—especially Burke—fully realized that the Colonists had outgrown the old dependence. The American Revolution was only the concrete point at which the foreseeable and foreseen event of independence took place. Though in actual form it was as unique as any historical happening, the Revolution was a natural and logical development. If the conflict over England's colonial policy had not precipitated the issue, something else would have done it—at the latest, one might guess, the physical unification of the country through the railroads.

Full self-government had become a foregone conclusion as soon as England had given the Colonists military self-government with their own troops under native commanders. The French and Indian War probably made eventual independence almost inevitable; and that war should rightly be regarded as fully as important in the history of American nationhood as the Declaration of Independence itself. There is a straight line from George Washington, the militia officer with his independent command in the French and Indian War, to George Washington, the Commander-in-Chief of the forces of the United States.

But as a European event the American Revolution was not foreseeable and foreseen. It reversed—first in England and then in the rest of Europe—a trend which had appeared to be inevitable, natural, and unchangeable. It defeated the rationalist liberals and their pupils, the Enlightened Despots, who had seemingly been irresistible and within an inch of complete and final victory. The American Revolution brought victory and power to a group which in Europe had been almost completely defeated and which was apparently dying out rapidly:

the anticentralist, antitotalitarian conservatives with their hostility to absolute and centralized government and their distrust of any ruler claiming perfection. It saved the autonomous common law from submersion under perfect law codes; and it re-established independent law courts. Above all, it reasserted the belief in the imperfection of man as the basis of freedom.

Had America not revolted against Enlightened Despotism there would hardly have been any freedom in the Europe of the nineteenth century. And the same would have been true if she had gone down before the armies of a rationalist and centralizing English king. There would hardly have been any effective English resistance against the French Revolution, and probably no national determination to fight it out with the aggressive totalitarianism of Napoleon. Above all, the justly celebrated English Constitution would not have survived to become for nineteenth-century Europe the symbol of freedom and of successful resistance against absolute tyranny.

That the thinly populated and remote American Colonies became independent was in itself of no great importance to the Western world of the late eighteenth and early nineteenth century. But in its effects upon Europe —as the defeat of the Enlightenment in the person of George III, as the basis for the emergence in England of the unenlightened but free conservatism of Burke against all apparent ratio, predictability, or probability —the American Revolution was the decisive historical event of the nineteenth century. It was the fountainhead and origin of the free mercantile society of the nineteenth century.

To avoid misunderstanding: It is not asserted here that Burke obtained his ideas or thoughts by reading the *Federalist* papers or from listening to Dr. Franklin— just as Jefferson, Madison, or Hamilton did not obtain their ideas from Burke or Blackstone. They probably thought quite independently of each other though their thoughts had common roots. It is even quite immaterial whether the American political thinkers of the Revolution knew Burke's speeches or whether he knew their essays. The one fact that matters is that the success of the American Revolution defeated the King of England and with it the entire Enlightenment. Without it Burke and the conservative counterrevolution could not have come to power.

Burke's ideas as well as those of the Founding Fathers were old ideas, common to all English and European tradition. There were many statesmen and writers on the Continent who shared them. But the American Revolution translated them into political action. It found institutions to realize them. It converted metaphysical reflections into concrete, responsible decisions.

The nineteenth century forgot not only that it owed its freedom to the principles of the American counterrevolution; it forgot that freedom has anything to do with basic principles. Increasingly its political discussion became confined to incidentals and details. Up to the last war—and even beyond it—there was a growing tendency to identify freedom and free society with refinements in technique. If anybody were to deduce the development of Western society from 1776 to 1930 solely by reading its political literature, he would inevitably conclude that freedom and society had been overtaken by a tremendous catastrophe—a sudden collapse into pre-Aristotelian barbarism. The descent from the political wisdom, knowledge and profundity of the generation of Burke, Rousseau, Jefferson, Hamilton, Madison, Herder, etc., to the mediocrity, shallowness, and ignorance of the political writers and thinkers of late Victorianism is so complete, so stunning, and so sudden as to be almost without parallel in the history of political thought. The distance from Madison to General Grant, Mark Hanna, and William Jennings Bryan, from Burke to Gladstone or to Joseph Chamberlain, from Herder to Treitschke or to the German *Socialdemocraten* of 1890, is almost too great to be measured.

This decline of the level of political thought is perhaps the greatest testimony to the work of the Founding Fathers; for the explanation of the collapse is that the generation of 1776 had built so well that their sons and grandsons could afford to forget the foundations and to concentrate on the interior decoration of the house they had inherited. It is only today that we must again think of first principles.

It is not a new assertion that the basis for all nineteenth-century freedom lay in the conservative movement which overcame the French Revolution. Nor is it a new discovery that, as far as Europe is concerned, this conservative movement was located in England. Before 1850 it was a commonplace of European political thought that England had found "the way out"—just as it became a commonplace later on to trace all nineteenth-century freedom to the French Revolution. But how did England overcome the French Revolution? What enabled her to withstand it and, at the same time, to develop without civil war and social collapse a free, mercantile society as alternative to the despotism of the French Revolution and of Napoleon? The stock answers to these questions attribute the English achievement to the British racial genius, the English Channel, or the English Constitution. But none of the three is an adequate answer.

Of the traditional answers we can most easily dismiss the racial-genius explanation. To attribute a historical development to the racial genius or the national character of a people is simply saying that we do not know the cause. There is such a thing as race and national character, but it explains nothing, if only because it cannot be defined and cannot be assumed to be incapable of change. Whether Neville Chamberlain or Winston Churchill more closely expresses the British national character is not only a moot, it is a silly question. Was Cromwell's totalitarian despotism more or less English than the wisdom and moderation of the settlement of 1688? Does the superstitious blasphemy of Henry VIII or the lucid piety of Thomas More characterize the Englishman? All of these men and events are very English and show traits, feelings, attitudes which are as alive today as they ever were. But what is English is the temper and temperament, not the principles, actions, or decisions. To say that it is typical for the Englishman to fight best with his back to the wall may be a true statement of national character; it is in any event a meaningful one. To say that representative government or free trade are in keeping with the English—or anybody else's—character is gibberish. And to say that the English are "naturally" opposed to revolution, because they "naturally" are law-abiding or because they "naturally" believe in gradual change, flies in the face of all historical fact. Prior to the French Revolution no other European country had as sanguinary, as revolutionary, as tumultuous a history as England.

There is more truth in the mechanistic explanation according to which the thirty miles of the Channel preserved England from the revolution. They certainly prevented England's defeat by the French armies and thus created the factual basis without which England's achievement would have been impossible. They were a condition of England's success—just as they have been a condition of England's political position since Caesar. But they did not create the new institutions of a free mercantile society.

The English Constitution too was a condition of the successful free solution without being the solution itself. It is perfectly true that the nineteenth-century freedom rests upon the Settlement of 1688, on the constitutional principles of the Whig party which Locke put into systematic form, on the common law and Chief Justice Coke, and ultimately on the Magna Charta. But these principles were not unique to England; they were common to all of Europe and the result of the constitutional development between the thirteenth and the seventeenth century. It is not only Magna Charta which has an exact counterpart in the constitutional history of every major European nation. The English Parliament before 1688 was also not very different from the *Etats Généraux* in France, the *Cortes* of Spain, the *Reichstag* and *Landstaende* in Germany. Common law, independent courts, city privileges and all the other traditional bulwarks of English freedom have their exact counterpart on the Continent. The Low Countries, Burgundy, and western and southern Germany were in 1550 or 1600 actually further along the road to political freedom and constitutional government than the England of the Tudors with their almost successful attempt to subvert the English Constitution.

If we want to talk about England's unique development, we cannot begin before 1688. Up to the Stuarts the development in England had been parallel to the development of the Continent. Although England escaped the Thirty Years' War which destroyed the free constitution of the old society on the Continent, Cromwell, the Commonwealth, and the Restoration did not bring any new solution and seemed eventually to lead in the same direction which the Continent had found under Richelieu, Mazarin or the Great Elector of Bradenburg-Prussia. The Settlement of 1688, however, was a complete break with the continental trend and a reestablishment of an English Constitution on non-absolutist principles.

What is hardly ever realized today is that eighty years later very little was left of this Constitution and England was apparently about to become an Enlightened Despotism like every other European country. On the eve of the American Revolution, Parliament had practically ceased to function as an organ of govern-

ment. Royal patronage commanded a permanent majority of the House of Commons. The King and his
ministers ruled almost as supremely as the King of
France. Administration had been centralized in the hands
of the King's cabinet—appointed by him and responsible only to him. Politics was almost synonymous with
court intrigues. The common law still stood, but it stood
also in France and Germany. And the same forces were
at work which on the Continent were about to lead to a
rationalist codification within a generation. The great
dazzling light of the English political scene in 1776 was
not Burke, not Pitt, not Blackstone, not even Adam
Smith. It was that most dangerous of all liberal totalitarians, Jeremy Bentham, who had a thousand schemes
to enslave the world for its own good. It is no accident
that Bentham expounded his social theories in a plan for
a model prison in which one man would at all times be
able to see the smallest movement of a thousand pris-
oners, and to control their most minute actions. And it
was Bentham who was "progressive" and "scientific"—
not the adherents to the principles of 1688 with their
apparently outmoded ideas of compromise and divided
powers.

If this sounds like an exaggeration, attention should
be given to the weakness of the forces opposing absolutism in England. We know how few "Old Whigs"
there were in England a decade after the Enlightenment,

in the person of George III, had been defeated by the American Colonists at Saratoga and Yorktown. At the beginning of the French Revolution, Burke stood virtually alone between the pro-Jacobines and the King's party which wanted a royal absolutism. Ten years earlier there had been even less strength in the conservative faction which was equally opposed to royal and demagogic tyrants. There were Burke, still a young, hardly known politician; the elder Pitt, out of power and favor; Blackstone, a teacher of the common law. Otherwise there were only reactionaries or liberal totalitarians— both equally opposed to the English Constitution and the English freedom. Without the American Revolution, Burke would hardly have achieved more than Herder and Moeser in Germany who, at the same time and with the same ideas, failed to find a conservative free society for Germany. Or he might have gone under like Fénelon who, fifty years earlier, had tried to prevent royal tyranny in France in the name of the old Christian freedom.

The American Revolution was the event which marked the turning of the absolutist and rationalist tide. Prior to 1776 English society, the society of 1688, had been disintegrating rapidly. The society which Hogarth drew, Lawrence Sterne described, Swift and Dr. Johnson castigated, was not a healthy and hardly a functioning society. True, there were no serfs in England as there were on the Continent. But there was an army of dispossessed:

victims of the Enclosures, victims of early industrialization, victims of rack-renting and of urban poverty. Nowhere on the Continent was there anything comparable
to the misery and squalor of the London slums with their
Gin Alleys, or to the horror of child labor in Manchester. Indeed, one of England's most popular economic and political writers of the time, Arthur Young,
was convinced—probably rightly—that the French peasant with all his feudal burdens was much better off than
the English small-holder or landless laborer.

The picture we have of England around 1770 is one
of stark corruption with an unpopular dynasty gobbling
up power through bribes and patronage, a mercenary
nobility willing, even eager, to be bought, a hostile middle class and a sullen almost desperate peasantry. It
was easy, perhaps deceptively easy, for the historian a
hundred years later to see in this society the germs of
England's strong and free nineteenth century. But the
contemporaries saw only a choice between revolutionary
catastrophe and royal enlightened absolutism.

It can never be proved whether George III and his
advisers welcomed the conflict with the Thirteen Colonies as the apparently easiest way to impose Enlightened
Despotism upon England. Burke apparently thought so.
But judging by ordinary political standards it is highly
unlikely that they had so deep and premeditated a plan.

Probably they had no plan at all; stupidity, confusion, greed, lack of judgment, and planlessness are far more common in politics than the conspiracies of supermen and the careful calculations of master-politicians which hardly exist outside of historical novels. And neither George III nor Lord North were supermen or master-politicians.

But if the King and his advisers had deliberately intended to impose Enlightened Despotism on England, they could not have hit upon a better scheme than to start by imposing it on America. The attack on the freedom and liberties of the Englishmen in the Colonies was bound to be popular at home where the Colonials were both disliked and envied. The legal position of the Thirteen Colonies was sufficiently obscure to lend to the attack on them a specious cloak of legality, and to make their legitimate resistance appear rebellion. They were weak, had never been united, were separated from each other by roadless wastes, by differences in social structure and political beliefs. And once a centralized royal absolutism had been imposed on them, the position of the central government would have become so strong, its resources so enormous, its prestige so great as to make resistance at home practically impossible.

There can be no doubt that the judgment of history is correct, and that both George III and Lord North were just shortsighted and selfish opportunists. Yet the most

Machiavellian, most cunning, most perspicacious political genius would not have acted differently in his attempt to impose his tyranny upon the British people. For the establishment of a centralized and absolute royal government over the Thirteen Colonies would have weakened the antitotalitarian opposition in the British Isles so much that it is hard to see how it could have maintained itself at all. And successful resistance of the Colonists against the foremost military and naval power of the age seemed to be practically impossible and was certainly entirely unexpected.

As it was, the failure of the royal plans defeated absolutism in England. In 1770 everything in England was moving increasingly fast toward Enlightened Despotism. In 1780 the antitotalitarian forces were in the saddle. The King had lost—never to regain the chance for absolute power. And the revolutionary competitors of the King, the Rousseauan totalitarians, who wanted to establish their tyranny, their absolutism, their centralized government in the place of royal tyranny and royal centralized government had lost out too. Neither the absolutism of the King nor that of the masses survived.

It was not only in America that the consent of the governed was made the basis for the limitation of the power of government. The principle became also victorious in England; the new constitution was actually not just a restoration of the parliamentary principles of 1688. Then the consent of the governed had been little more than an expedient to prevent civil war. The sum of wisdom of the "Trimmers" who had written the Constitution of the Glorious Revolution had been to avoid conflicts and to choose the way of least resistance. In this form, limited government had not only fallen into almost complete disuse in practice. It had also almost been given up in theory; and by 1770 it had come to be considered "unscientific," "contrary to nature," "abhorrent" to philosophy and logic. After the successful resistance of the Colonists it came back into actual power in the persons of Pitt and Burke. And in the new form it rested on a basic principle of freedom.

Every single one of the free institutions of England's nineteenth-century political system actually traces back to the short tenure of office of the "Old Whigs" who came to power because they had opposed the war with the Thirteen Colonies. They introduced ministerial responsibility to Parliament, and the cabinet system. They founded the modern party system and the civil service. And they defined the relationship between Crown and Parliament. The England of 1790 was not a very healthy and certainly not an ideal society. But it had found the basic frame for a new free society. And that frame was the principles of the "Old Whigs" who had been practically destroyed before the American Revolution, and who were not only revived but put into power by the successful resistance of the Colonists.

The decisive impact of the ideas and principles of 1776 shows best in a comparison between England and the Continent of Europe. In England during the nineteenth century both Liberals and Conservatives based themselves on the same principles of a free society. Their conflict was over the limitations of freedom, not over freedom itself. It was the old conflict between "authoritarianism" and "individualism," but not a conflict over the essence or meaning of freedom itself.

The party on the Continent that called itself "Liberal" was rationalist and absolutist; and it was completely opposed to any real freedom. The so-called Conservatives were equally rationalist and absolutist though their rationalism was a reactionary one. The nineteenth-century Continental Liberal was a product of the French Revolution; the Conservative was in reality a survival from the days of Enlightened Despotism. He was the rationalist totalitarian of yesterday.

There was indeed a conservative movement on the Continent of Europe during the nineteenth century which was based on the same ideas which in the Founding Fathers and in Burke had become victorious. The European counterpart was the romantic movement. In its best representatives, especially in the great French political romanticists of 1820, it reached a lucidity and profundity which can stand comparison with the best work of the American writers. The Romantic movement had a tremendous influence upon the arts and sciences; it may be called the father of all comparative and of all biological sciences. But politically it was completely ineffective. It could only project its ideas of freedom backward into the romantic mirage of the Middle Ages. But it could not create a functioning free nineteenth-century society, for it was caught between the rival absolutisms of rationalist radicalism and rationalist reaction.

Whatever freedom the Continent of Europe enjoyed during the nineteenth century was a result of the inability of either of these opposing absolutist creeds to establish its dictatorship over the other. Freedom was not the accepted basis. It was the accidental by-product of armed truce between two equally strong and equally totalitarian enemies. In England and America freedom was of the essence, and the basis for party conflicts. On the Continent freedom was negative—the absence of party tyranny. It existed only because either side loved the opposition even less than it loved freedom.

The history of any major Continental country proves this thesis; but that of France is most illustrative because most spectacular. It is usually forgotten by those who cannot understand the France of Vichy that, for more than a hundred years after 1789, France was the most unstable country in Europe and always either preparing for, or recovering from, a revolution in which one absolutist faction tried to suppress the other and to establish its own tyranny. Only between these revolutions or near-revolutions when either side was exhausted, or when forces were equally matched, was there not only peace but freedom in France. Two of these upheavals were violent: that of 1848 and the sanguinary Commune of 1870. Four more brought civil war uncomfortably close: the coup d'état of Napoleon III, the abortive plot of Marshal MacMahon to restore the monarchy, the plot of General Boulanger to establish a personal, military dictatorship, and, finally, the Dreyfus affair. Only after this last attempt on the part of the absolutists of the Right—just barely foiled by the resistance of the Left—did French politics cease to be the politics of imminent or actual civil war. It had been shown conclusively that neither side could win. The "Dreyfusards"—conservative men with a radical conscience, as they have been called not ineptly—really accepted and wanted freedom. What they got was an armed truce between irreconcilable camps, as the last years and especially the years of the Front Populaire, Laval and Pétain have shown only too clearly.

2.

It is customary, especially in America, to view the achievements of 1776 and 1787 in exclusively legal terms. And the formulation of the American Constitution, the restoration and rejuvenation of the English Constitution, are indeed the most tangible monuments of the conservative counterrevolution. But it also laid the basis for the growth of extra-legal, extra-constitutional institutions for a hundred years afterward. It provided the principles on which they were based, the directions which they took, and the goal for which they aimed. In actual political and social life these extra-legal and extra-constitutional institutions were at least as important as the constitutions themselves.

Constitutions are a frame; they are a legal skeleton and nothing else. They set the limits for the political powers and the rules of procedure for their exercise. But they cannot organize society. The Founding Fathers have no greater claim to wisdom than that they never tried to do by legal and constitutional means what can be done only through social institutions. They never tried to manufacture institutions. They refused to impose an institutional strait jacket upon posterity. But in solving their day-to-day problems they developed the principles of a free society and of free government so firmly that the succeeding generations could build on their foundation. There were tremendous changes in the fabric of society during the century after the conservative counterrevolution. In both America and England the institutions on which political life centered in 1876 were completely different from those of 1776. They were also different from anything the generation of 1776 had foreseen or would have expected. But without exception these new institutions were based on the principles of a free government and a free society as developed by the conservative counterrevolution.

In the United States there is in the first place the system of two parties based not upon ideological and perfectionist programs but upon traditions and local organization and permanent machines. Contrary to all party organization in Europe, the American political party is not a central and centralized body primarily concerned with conquering the central government. In spite of the tremendous uproar of presidential and congressional elections, the main interest of the party politicians centers on local city, county and state affairs. The national party is actually a holding corporation for very limited purposes. The local boss in city, county, and state is interested in national affairs and national elections only insofar as they tend to affect his own bailiwick. But the center of his power and interest remains local.

Accordingly, the national contests every two or four

years are disturbances for the local machines rather than—as in Europe—their primary raison d'etre. The local organizations can survive—and survive well—without control of the central power. The Democratic party survived out of power far longer than any large European party could possibly have sustained itself in opposition. There is no machine politician in the United States—even in this age of growing central power—who would not rather have his party lose the presidency and gain control of all the key cities, than gain the presidency but lose locally.

With their strength in the local organizations, the American parties are strongly anticentralist. The president is nominally the party chief, but no president has ever lived at peace with his party, except by submitting to its anticentralist demands. By the same token no strong president has ever grown out of the "regular" party machine with its preoccupation with local affairs and "strategy." Thus the party, while an instrument to win power at the center, has seldom been able to win it for itself. It has therefore always been suspicious of, and opposed to, any extension of central power and any encroachment upon local autonomy.

With its center in local issues and with its "party line" a compromise between many conflicting, local and regional beliefs, the American party has never become committed to an "all or nothing" program. Being unideological, it can offer scope to any political belief, however extreme. It thus makes unnecessary and almost impossible the growth of extremist movements outside of party ranks. Yet, being free from ideological commitments, it can embody—and has done so—any popular demand once it has rallied sufficient popular support. It thus prevents—or at least slows down—sudden and radical shifts in policy. But it provides a vehicle for any and every program that becomes general.

In fine, the American party has not only been an extremely conservative institution—anticentral and anti-authoritarian, regional and undogmatic; it has also been one of the most effective means of preventing government from becoming absolute. The party is in the state but not of the state. It has no counterpart in any modern European institution. The only parallels in Europe would be the estates of the late Middle Ages—like the American party anticentralist, regional and nonideological, autonomous corporations.

Another very important though completely extralegal safeguard of freedom in America has been the divorce of political from socio-economic power and standing. It may be true that the corruption of professional politics was the original reason that "respectable" people retired from political life. It is more likely that the corruption is an effect, not a cause, of the withdrawal of the gentleman from the arena into the counting house. In any case, the resulting lack of social esteem and standing of the profession of politics has led to a split between the political ruling class and the social ruling class which has prevented any one group from becoming *the* ruling class. And the contempt for the machine politicians has made it easy to throw out any political leader who tried to make his tenure permament.

The American experience has amply borne out the old saying that a corrupt ruler who can be thrown out is infinitely preferable to an honest "enlightened" and unselfish despot who, by virtue of these very qualities, is so respected as to become irremovable. And—contrary to general American belief—the experience with noncorrupt, "clean," municipal and provincial governments in Germany, France, or England does not make the price paid for the unintentional but tangible blessings of corruption appear to have been too high.

Above all, however, American freedom has been resting on American invisible self-government. A considerable part of governmental functions in the United States has been exercised by spontaneous, autonomous, and voluntary associations locally and regionally. It cannot be called a new development, for its roots are in the Colonial past, if not in medieval England. But in the spontaneous, unorganized form in which it became effective in nineteenth-century America, invisible self-government grew out of the principles of 1776. The churches and the chambers of commerce, the Rotarians, the parent-teachers associations, etc., are not conscious that they discharge quasi-governmental functions; nor is the individual member aware of the fact that he takes part in spontaneous community government. Yet these associations, which are unique to the United States, do govern. They set community standards, discharge community functions, mold public opinion, and force or prevent community action. A man who wants to settle as a lawyer, doctor, or businessman in an English small town tries to get the support and moral backing of the "squire" and of the "gentry"; without it he is lost. In Germany—before Hitler—he had to get the support of the government officials on the spot: the local judge, the police chief, the provincial governor, and so on. In this country, a newcomer tries to get access to Rotary, the chamber of commerce, a particular church congregation, etc. These spontaneous and voluntary associations are perhaps the strongest antitotalitarian force extant in the present world.

On the basis of this analysis it appears that the freedom America has been enjoying cannot wholly or even largely be attributed to the frontier and to continental expansion. Indeed, there is perhaps no more vicious thesis than that freedom was a by-product of the frontier—except its European counterpart according to which imperialist expansion was the basis of England's and Europe's freedom during the nineteenth century. Both statements imply that there can be no freedom without a frontier or without colonial expansion—in other words, that there can be no freedom today.

It is at least arguable that the frontier and the phenomenal material and geographical expansion of America which resulted were as much of a strain on freedom as a help. Of course, the frontier was a tremendous safety valve—both for America and for Europe. It bred a spirit of equality and, more important, of an equal chance for everybody to become unequal—that is, privileged—which went far to make the promises of 1776 come true. But, on the other hand, the frontier and its rapid advance made inevitable the rise of the monopolistic "trust," the big railroad, timber, steel or land corporation with its tremendous dangers to freedom. The problems it imposed on a new nation had hardly ever been met before.

It is highly symptomatic that American independent political thinking ceased almost completely as soon as the explosive development of the frontier started in the middle forties. There have been no greater and no more original political thinkers in modern Europe than were produced by the first generation of American independence: Jefferson, Hamilton, Madison, and Marshall. Even the second-rate men of those days, Monroe, Gallatin, the two Adamses, were respectable political philosophers in their own right. And, though the men of the next generation were a great deal smaller, there were still giants in Jackson, Webster, Clay, Calhoun, and the grossly underrated Van Buren.

After that what may be called the original stream of American political thinking disappeared; and it did not come out of its cave till the frontier was closing. Lincoln's tragic figure stands alone. But even Lincoln had no political philosophy. His greatness lies in his humanity. Before the time of Populism and of Wilson the physical strain of expansion was apparently too great to allow political thinking.

The one thing about the frontier that can be said with certainty is that the basis of American freedom was broad enough to make such unexpected expansion possible. It was firm enough to stand the strain. The principles were sound enough to neutralize all that was potentially unfree and absolutist in the frontier and in the rapid economic and geographic expansion; and they released all the forces in the expansion that were potentially capable of strengthening freedom.

Beginning with the Northwestern Ordinance the history of American expansion is the greatest story of the potential and inherent possibilities of free government.

But there is little in this story to justify the belief that free government must have rapid material expansion, or that such expansion is the only task free government can master.

As far as English freedom during the nineteenth century is concerned, the two slogans which everybody has heard are "parliamentary sovereignty" and "majority government." Actually the English political system of the nineteenth century consisted largely of the limitations of parliamentary sovereignty and of majority government. England really had minority rule limited by majority consent.

The concrete political institutions through which these aims were realized were: the two-party system which made the opposition an integral part of the government, the emergence of the cabinet and the independent civil service.

It might be said—though not without exaggeration— that the English Constitution during the nineteenth century could have worked without a government but not without an opposition. The ever-present possibility of an *alternative* government was actually the decisive fact of English political life. The will of the majority could never be final or absolute, for the dissenting will of the minority in opposition was as much the will of the British people and of the British government as the will of the majority in power.

The English—and the American—systems have been criticized as "undemocratic." It is said that they prevent the absolute rule of the majority. But that is not only their function but also their main justification. By preventing absolute rule they safeguard freedom. Equally is it praise for the two-party system and not criticism to say that it prevents small groups from becoming effective.

Nothing is more salutary than the compulsion for new ideas and new leaders to fight their way through existing and working large parties. It forces the new to prove itself better and more effective than the old before it is allowed to supplant the old. To facilitate small factions and fractions destroys parliamentary government. It leads to a hopeless subdivision of political units which makes orderly government almost impossible. It always gives minuscule groups, representing nobody but themselves, a decisive position, a bargaining strength, a power and a freedom of access to the public purse which are out of all proportion to its real following in the population. The two-party system is not only a safeguard against majority tyranny but also against minority tyranny.*

---

* Though it is a distortion to regard proportional representation as the sole or main cause of the rise of Hitlerism or of the fall of France,

The limitation of majority rule through the two-party system was only one factor in the institutional machinery through which the government of England was divided and limited. A second factor was cabinet government, or, more precisely, the emergence of the prime minister. In effect, though not in law, the office of prime minister as it first emerged in the elder Pitt and as it has remained unchanged since Peel, derives its power not from Parliament but from the people. The prime minister is elected by the people; that the voter votes for his local member of Parliament and not for Disraeli, Gladstone or Asquith often had little more meaning than that the American voter legally casts his vote for a member of the Electoral College, not for the presidential candidate directly. Though elected indirectly, the prime minister was actually directly empowered to take charge of the executive branch of the government. He was limited by the requirement of parliamentary confidence. He was subject to recall in a general election every five years, if not earlier. But his power was in fact original and not derived power.

This fact which every prime minister understood,

I agree with Dr. F. A. Hermens and other defenders of the two-party system that the multi-party system and the ease with which extreme groups could obtain representation were among the main causes of the weakness of popular government on the Continent of Europe. Here again European rationalism sacrificed freedom to the quest for perfection.

though it is not to be found in any textbook of English constitutional law, meant an effective division of powers and functions—an effective system of "checks and balances." In the first place, it severely limited the scope and power of Parliament. To oppose the policy of a prime minister was not as easy a matter as it was in France or in Republican Germany, where prime ministers were the creatures of Parliament. It was also a more difficult and more dangerous matter than the opposition of an American Congress to a president, which does not impose upon Congress the responsibility to find an alternative. Opposition to a prime minister who, in effect, was elected by the people, imposed the responsibility upon Parliament to find an alternative at least as acceptable to the people. A prime minister defeated in Parliament could always call upon the electorate to sustain him; or he could turn to the leader of the opposition and force him to obtain the direct endorsement of the people. In either case, interference by Parliament was extremely hazardous, could only be risked over principal issues, and could only be undertaken—legally and actually—as a last resort. Cabinet government thus virtually removed the greater part of executive policy from the power and function of Parliament. At the same time, the need for parliamentary sanction constituted a severe limitation upon the executive.

Opposition and the prime minister may be said to be

organs of Parliament—though their main function was to prevent parliamentary absolutism. The civil service, however, is entirely independent of Parliament. It clearly and indisputably constituted a limitation of parliamentary power from the outside.

The civil service in the form in which it gradually developed in Great Britain during the nineteenth century, was a co-ruler with autonomous power, checked and balanced by Parliament just as much as it checked and balanced Parliament. But it was not controlled, created or dependent upon Parliament—except in legal fiction. Altogether the British civil service can be said to have exercised a function very similar to that exercised in the United States by the courts. It made sure that there was no sudden break in the continuity of development; it provided the main course underlying all temporary deviations, and it nullified parliamentary or executive encroachments upon established principles.

Every senior civil servant was expected as a matter of routine to prepare at the same time alternative policies for the alternating parties. This ensured automatically that the two alternative proposals for the same situation would not differ in basic principle. Permanence of tenure, independence from both Parliament and the cabinet, and the existence of a permanent undersecretary as the real chief of each department, made the civil service an effective control and check of both Parliament and cabinet. The budgetary power of Parliament and the power of the cabinet to lay down the broad political frame for the work of each department checked and limited in turn the civil service.

As long as the civil service fulfilled nothing but this original function, the often heard criticism that it lacked imagination and initiative was unjustified. Insofar as the civil service had political functions, it acted as an arbiter with semijudicial powers. It is not the business of a judge to imagine and initiate, but to restrain and to propitiate. Initiative and imagination, political leadership and vision had to come from Parliament or from the cabinet. The civil service had to see that such initiative and imagination were practical and in accordance with the basic principles of continuous government. It had what in effect amounted to a right and duty of judicial review by administrative process. But the very fact that a permanent undersecretary would have been remiss in his duty had he failed to prepare legislation for both the conservative and the liberal minister meant that he could not have taken the initiative himself without abandoning his real task.

This, of course, holds true only for the period when the civil service had this function as one branch of the government, controlled by and controlling the others. It is no longer true today when the civil service has in many respects become *the* government. This development of the political power of the bureaucracy which has cut down the power and function of both, Parliament and the cabinet, began around 1900. It is the most dangerous trend in English political life. It has almost destroyed the English Constitution and has created— for the first time in 175 years—a real danger of a centralized absolute despotism in Britain.

It is important to realize that the principles of the conservative counterrevolution resulted in a free society in the United States and in England although these two countries were dissimilar to start with. Though the American of 1776 was of the same racial stock as his contemporary in England, although he spoke the same language, had the same laws and, by and large, the same political tradition, he was sufficiently far removed from the mother country to rule out the attempt to explain the nineteenth-century free society in these two countries by the "racial genius" or the "political wisdom" of one race or nation.

It is not only true that the actual social and physical reality, the patterns of thought and of behavior, the concrete problems and the concrete answers given in these two countries during the nineteenth century were completely different. The United States also moved away from England and from Europe during the entire century at an increasing pace as a result of the Revolution and of the westward movement which started soon afterward. The America of 1917, that came in to decide the greatest European war since Napoleon, was further away from Europe than the America of the colonial towns, of Jefferson, Dr. Franklin, George Washington, and John Adams. Steamboats, transatlantic cables and wireless by their very facility only tended to make contacts more superficial and passing than they had been in the days of the sailing vessel.

Every succeeding generation of Americans since the Revolution has been further away from England—or for that matter, from Europe—than its predecessors. Jackson and Clay were living at greater social and mental distance from Europe than John Quincy Adams or Daniel Webster—both of whom can be imagined as Englishmen though as Englishmen of the eighteenth century. Lincoln, Grant, Andrew Johnson, the railroad builders were even further away from Europe than Jackson and Clay. And with the next generation—that of Theodore Roosevelt and Woodrow Wilson, of Rockefeller, Morgan and Carnegie, Henry Adams and Lincoln Steffens— the United States was producing a type of leader and a mental and social climate which, for better or worse, was simply not imaginable in any European society— least of all in the England of 1900. There is a good deal of truth in the aphorism current among English newspaper correspondents that the United States had traveled

so far away from Europe in mentality, customs and institutions as to have become almost comprehensible to a
European. And it is a commonplace among writers and
journalists who have to report on American developments for English readers (as I did for several years)
that the common written language is more a handicap
than a help, as it creates the illusion—fatal to a real
understanding—that words and sentences have the same
emotional and intellectual significance, the same associations and overtones, on either side of the Atlantic.

But the difference between these two countries only
emphasizes the universality of the principles which both
adopted. Starting from a different basis, wrestling with
completely different realities, working in different social
and emotional climates, both countries succeeded in developing a free mercantile society. However much they
differed, they both took as their starting point that no
man or group of men is perfect or in possession of
Absolute Truth and Absolute Reason. And both the
American Founding Fathers and the radical Conservatives in England believed in mixed government; in the
consent of the governed as one, and in individual property rights as the other, limitation of government; in the
separation of government in the political sphere from
rule in the social sphere.

3.

The American and English conservatives of 1776 and
1787 shared not only the principles; they also had in
common the method which they used to develop a functioning society on a free basis. They both used it the
same way and gave it the same consideration and the
same importance.

The method of the conservative counterrevolution is
just as important for us today as its principles—perhaps
even more so. A good many political writers and thinkers
today believe that principles are everything and that no
such thing as method is required. This is a basic misunderstanding of the nature of politics and of political
action which the generation of 1776 never would have
made. They knew that principles without institutional
realization are just as ineffective politically—and as
vicious for the social order—as institutions without principles. Accordingly, method was as important to them
as principles. And their success was just as much due to
their method as to their principles.

Their method consisted in the last analysis of three
parts:

In the first place, while conservative, they did not
restore nor intend to restore. They never did idealize
the past; and they had no illusions about the present in
which they lived. They knew that the social reality had

changed. They would never have conceived their task as anything but the integration of the new society on the basis of the old principles; never would they have countenanced any attempt to undo what had happened.

It is their unconditional refusal to restore which has made the Founding Fathers appear radical, and which has obscured the essentially conservative character of their work. Their social analysis was indeed radical—extremely radical. They never accepted the polite social conventions or the wishful restoration dreams which were based on the assumption that the old society was still functioning whereas in effect it had disappeared. It has often been remarked that in his factual analysis Burke agrees with Rousseau to an amazing extent. And a good many people have been surprised that, with the same evaluation of the facts as basis, he should have come to the opposite political conclusions. But the true conservative always agrees with the true revolutionary on the facts. Both understand, as neither Reactionary nor Liberal does, the nature of politics and of society. It is only on principles that they disagree; the one wants to create or to maintain freedom, the other to destroy it. But the conservative is no less conservative for being realistic about facts. And the generation of 1776 and 1787 saw the essence of their conservatism in the fact that they did not intend to restore. For restoration is just as violent and absolutist as revolution.

The Founding Fathers in America and the radical conservatives in England were thus conservatives of the present and future, rather than conservatives of the past. They knew that their social reality was that of a mercantile system, while their social institutions were pre-mercantile. Their method was to start with this fact and to develop a free and functioning mercantile society. They wanted to solve the future, not the past, to overcome the next and not the last revolution.

The second basic characteristic of their method was that they did not believe in blueprints or panaceae. They believed in a broad frame of general principles; and there they admitted of no compromise. But they knew that an institutional solution is acceptable only if it works; that is, if it solves an actual social problem. They also knew that practically every concrete institutional tool can be made to serve practically every ideal aim. They were doctrinaire in their dogmas, but extremely pragmatic in their day-to-day politics. They did not try to erect an ideal or a complete structure; they were even willing to contradict themselves in the details of actual solutions. All they wanted was a solution that would do the job in hand—provided it could be fitted into the broad frame of principles.

This statement will be accepted readily enough as far as England is concerned. Though England, the home of the great utopias, was the most doctrinaire country in Europe in the two centuries before 1700, Burke's opposition to dogmatism has become the basis of English politics. It has even been driven so far as to become "muddling through"—the *reductio ad absurdum* of Burke's attitude in which the fear of dogmatism leads to having no principles at all.

For the United States, however, it may be argued that the Founding Fathers did indeed set up a blueprint: the Constitution. But the wisdom of the Constitution lies not in the extent to which it lays down rules, but in its restraint. It contains a few basic principles, sets up a few basic institutions and lays down a few simple procedural rules. The members of the Philadelphia Convention opposed the inclusion of the Bill of Rights in the Constitution not so much out of hostility to its provisions as from an aversion against mortgaging the future. Yet the provisions of the Bill of Rights are largely negative in character and lay down only what ought not, rather than what ought, to be done. The classic example of both, the method of the Founding Fathers, and its success, is the Northwestern Ordinance. This document provided the legal basis for the whole westward movement and for the entirely new and highly successful method of organizing territories and creating new states. Yet it never wanted to be more than an ad hoc solution of an urgent, actual problem. Its makers neither envisaged nor expected what actually happened on the frontier within twenty-five years; all they did was to develop immediate piecemeal institutions and to fit them loosely into a wide frame of principles.

The wisdom of this approach can be amply proved by the actual experience of the generation of 1776. There were at least three men of unusual foresight and exceptional ability to see into the future. Jefferson was the only man in the America of 1800 who had a dim foreboding of the westward push which was to carry white settlement across the continent in less than a century. His political ideas were based on a faint vision of the great inland empire on the upper Mississippi that was to rise fifty years later. Yet he completely and utterly failed to see the rising tide of industrialization—though the railroad was the very thing which made his rural vision come true.

Hamilton, on the other hand, only saw industrialization. He was not only the one American, he was the only man of his generation—and of the next—who had an industrial vision. Yet he saw America forever bordered by the Appalachians and confined to the immediate hinterland of the great trading cities on the Atlantic Seaboard. Burke realized that international trade was going to be the basis of England's prosperity in the future. But he did not see that industry would be the basis of this trade or that English agriculture would have to be sacrificed to it.

Not a single one of the Constitution makers in Philadelphia saw that within forty years slavery would become the great issue, endangering the very union they built. All expected it to die a speedy and apparently inevitable death. Altogether there were only a very few men who foresaw even a minute fraction of the great developments that were just about to happen, and no one who saw them all. Yet theirs was not an unusually bad but an unusually good guessing average.

The generation of 1776 and 1787 was just as unable to foresee what was to become of their solutions. Burke himself believed that the English Constitution and the English freedom rested on the juxtaposition of House of Commons, House of Lords and the Crown. He would have said that the collapse of the independent political power of the Lords and of the Crown—both substantially completed with the Reform Bill of 1832—would have meant the end of English freedom. He was in favor of a legal system under which the Common Law would override parliamentary acts—that is, a system under which the courts could have declared acts of Parliament unconstitutional. In reality Parliament became the supreme lawgiver. The irony of the situation lies in the fact that the real safeguards of English freedom in the nineteenth century—the two-party system, the civil service and the responsible cabinet under a prime minister —all trace back to Burke who fathered the first two and assisted in the birth of the third. Yet he never saw their basic importance.

Similarly, in the United States the main dispute in the Constitutional Convention was between big and small states. If there was one thing of which the Constitution makers were prouder than the bit of political arithmetic with which they settled the big state–small state issue, it was the neat mathematical equation of the Electoral College which was to elect the president. The issue between big and small states never came up again; and the Electoral College never functioned. But no one in Philadelphia foresaw the tremendous importance of judicial review, if, indeed, they foresaw the right of judicial review at all. And they would all have abhorred the party system which became so vital and unique a part of American political life and so important a bulwark of freedom. It is significant and instructive that both judicial review and the party system came in as ad hoc political moves to solve a practical problem; the first as a move of party politics to fight the Jeffersonian trend, the second to elect Jackson against the old-line politicians.

Neither the Americans nor the English—with the single exception of Hamilton—foresaw the rise of the autonomous rule in the economic sphere. Both saw property as a legitimate basis of power and as a limitation on the government. Both believed in the divorce of political and social rule. Both limited the sphere of political government and thus made possible the rise of the rule in the economic sphere as an autonomous rule. But Burke—at the very time when the first of the great London banking houses were coming to the fore— thought with Jefferson that the economic rule would lie with the landowner.

The final point in the method of the conservative counterrevolution is what Burke called "prescription." That has nothing to do with the "sacredness of tradition." Burke himself ruthlessly discarded traditions and precedents when they did not work. Prescription is the expression in the field of political method of the principle of human imperfection. It simply says that man cannot foresee the future. He does not know where he goes. The only thing he can possibly know and understand is the actual society which has grown historically. Hence he must take existing social and political reality, rather than an ideal society, as the basis for his political and social activities. Man can never invent perfect institutional tools. Hence he had better rely upon old tools than try to invent new ones to do an ideal job. We know how an old tool works, what it can do and what it cannot do, how to use it and how far to trust it. And not only do we not know anything about the new tools; if they are hawked about as perfect tools we can be reasonably certain that they will work less well than the old ones which nobody expected or claimed to be perfect.

Prescription is not only the expression of the belief in human imperfection. It is not only the expression of that awareness that all society is the result of long historical growth which distinguishes the statesman from the mere politician. It is also a principle of economy; it teaches one to prefer the simple, cheap and common to the complicated, costly and shiny innovation. It is common sense pitted against Absolute Reason, experience and conscientiousness against superficial brilliance. It is plodding, pedestrian and not spectacular—but dependable.

The great practitioners of this principle were not so much the English as the American Founding Fathers. A vast amount of research has been done to show how completely they depended upon the institutions that had proved workable and dependable in colonial government and administration, upon past experience and tried tools. A good deal of this research has been done in a "debunking" mood with the object of showing that the Constitution makers were too dull and narrow to invent anything. This is, of course, as untenable as the proud belief of past generations that the America of 1788 had sprung fully armed out of the brains of the members of the Constitutional Convention. Actually, the caution with which the Founding Fathers avoided new and untried institutional constructions at a time of great stress and crisis is one of their greatest claims to wisdom and to our gratitude. They knew that they could use only what they had; and they also knew that the future has always started in the past and that it is the job of the statesman to decide which part of an imperfect past to stretch into a better future rather than to try to find the secret of perpetual political motion—or of perpetual political standstill.

The rise of an industrial system which cannot be organized socially by the mercantile society of the nineteenth century has destroyed—or at least seriously weakened—many of the most important parts of the achievements of 1776 and 1787. The nineteenth-century separation of political government and social rule—the great new safeguard of freedom—is almost gone. It is not being destroyed by a conspiracy or by mistakes. It has not failed because modern society is too "complex." It has been disappearing because the institutions of the mercantile society cannot organize the power in the industrial system. There must be a functioning legitimate rule in the socially constitutive sphere. But the market cannot supply it in the modern industrial corporation. Hence, central government has been moving in by default. And, as a consequence, we see today everywhere the rise of the centralized, uncontrollable and absolute bureaucracy which to the conservatives of 1776 was the supreme danger.

At the same time and for the same reason, self-government has been degenerating; it has almost disappeared. Popular government instead of being the vehicle to realize self-government, instead of being the institutional form for the individual's responsible decision, has largely become the means by which the individual escapes responsibility and decision. It has become the mechanism through which the individual shifts responsibility and decision from his own shoulders to those of people "paid to do the job"—the experts, the bureaucracy, finally a Fuehrer. Instead of self-government, we have largely today majority rule. Unless we create new institutions of self-government, we shall have the rule of the masses tomorrow; and the masses can only rule through, and be governed by, the tyrant.

The concrete society which the generation of 1776 built has largely broken down, and we must develop a new industrial society today. But both, the principles and the method of the conservative counterrevolution, still stand. If we want a free society, we can reach it only by adopting the same basic principles. The concrete social institutions of the future will be as different from those founded in 1776 and 1787 as they in turn were different from the institutions of the seventeenth or the eighteenth century. But if they are to be institutions of a free and a functioning society, the way to develop them is to use the same method as the generation of 1776: awareness that we cannot restore and that we have to accept the new industrial reality rather than try to go back to the old preindustrial mercantile system: willingness to forego blueprints and panaceae and to be content with the humble and less brilliant task of finding workable solutions—piecemeal and imperfect—for immediate problems; and knowledge that we can use only what we have, and that we have to start where we are, not where we want to go.

The conservative counterrevolution of 1776 and 1787 achieved what has probably never been achieved before in Western history: the development of a new society with new values, new beliefs, new powers and a new social integration without social revolution, without decades of civil war, without totalitarian tyranny. It not only overcame the totalitarian revolution by offering a free and functioning social and political alternative; it developed this alternative without itself becoming entangled in totalitarianism and absolutism. It built so well that its mercantile society could for a hundred years contain an ever-growing industrial system which was opposed to everything the mercantile society stood for and depended upon.

Our task today may seem bigger and more difficult than that of the generation of 1776—though we probably tend to underestimate their difficulties since we know the answers, and to overestimate our difficulties since we do not know what is to happen. But it is certain that we can hope to achieve our task only if we base ourselves on the principles and depend upon the methods which the generation of 1776 bequeathed to us.

CHAPTER NINE

A CONSERVATIVE APPROACH

IF the free industrial society is to be developed in a free, nonrevolutionary, nontotalitarian way, there is only one country that can do it today: the United States.

That the twentieth century is to be the "American Century" has recently become a popular catch phrase in the United States. It is certainly true that the United States can never again afford not to engage in power politics, not to develop lasting strategic concepts, not to determine where her strategic and military borders lie and which territories cannot be allowed to fall under the control of a potential enemy. It is also certain that both traditional American attitudes toward foreign affairs are obsolete, if not defunct. Both isolationism and interventionism assumed implicitly that the United States can decide whether she wants to be a participant in international affairs or not. Now that the United States has become the central power of the Western world, if not of the whole globe, there is no longer such a decision. America will have to take a stand whenever a power tries to assume hegemony on any continent—

even when there is nothing more than a change in international power relations.

It is extremely probable that America will extend her sphere of influence, expand her political and military radius, and take the lead in economic or social developments abroad—in short, that the United States of America will have to be an imperial, if not an imperialist power. All this is simply saying that the United States is a great power and cannot disregard the fact any longer. Politics cannot exist in the realm of ideas alone. The main task is to translate ideas into institutional reality; and the tool is power. The British in the past have often been attacked—rather stupidly—for "saying Christ and meaning Cotton." It would be infinitely worse if the United States as a world power were to say "Cotton" but to mean "Christ." In the past Americans have only too often been guilty of this dangerous inverse hypocrisy; they have striven after lofty ideals while pretending, even to themselves, that they wanted nothing but material and "practical" gain.

The task of the statesman is not to forget physical reality but to organize it for the fulfillment of his beliefs and concepts; and one indispensable requirement of such organization is that it work. The "idealist in politics" will always make a fool of himself and of the people who trust him. And the "politician" who sees nothing but organization never knows what he is striving for. The statesman who alone can be truly successful in politics can solve pragmatic problems of power and organization as well as the trickiest politician without ever giving up or compromising his basic principles. He never loses sight of the fact that ideal aims can be fulfilled only through institutional organization. On the other hand, he knows that principles, while not determining how to do things, decide what one does and why.

In conclusion, the United States as a world power—perhaps as *the* world power—will certainly have to use her power politically; that is, as power. But if the American century means nothing except the material predominance of the United States, it will be a wasted century. Some people today seem to think that it is the destiny of the United States to out-Nazi the Nazis in world conquest and to substitute the Yankee as the master race for Hitler's Nordics; some even call that "fighting for democracy." But this way would not lead to America's strength and greatness but only to her downfall. It would also not lead to a solution of the basic social crisis of which this war is but an effect. If the twentieth century is to have a free and functioning industrial society, the United States will have to solve the great problems of principles and institutions which today demand a solution. Then indeed the twentieth century will become an American century.

Of course, the nineteenth century was far more of an

American century than is commonly realized. The settlement of the North-American Continent was not only the greatest single achievement of the last century; the possibility of emigration to the free soil and the equal opportunities of the United States were the safety valves —both in a literal and a metaphysical sense—which kept the European social system from blowing up. Above all, the American Revolution, the conservative counterrevolution of 1776 and 1787, made possible the victory of the conservative forces in England who found the transition to the free mercantile society of the nineteenth century, and who overcame materially and spiritually the totalitarianism of the French Revolution. Yet withal, the United States during the nineteenth century was the periphery rather than the center of the Western world. The American Revolution released the forces in England which brought forth the new basis; it did not create them. The frontier made possible the growth and expansion of the European system by absorbing those the latter dispossessed and drove out. But the motor of Western development was in Europe, and more specifically in Great Britain.

In our time the driving forces, the basic beliefs and institutions, will have to be in the United States and will have to radiate from here. Even if England should find the conservative transition to an industrial society —and there are many promising signs in wartime England today—her counterrevolution will be successful only if it releases conservative forces in America. For the United States has become the strategic, political and economic center of international gravity. She has the most highly developed, most advanced and most powerful industrial mass-production system. Whatever social and political industrial order America develops, the other industrial countries will have to follow—provided that America develops a functioning industrial order.

The totalitarian powers were absolutely correct in their conviction—ever since they started on the road to world conquest—that the United States is their ultimate, their real enemy. It is true in a material sense; it is even truer in a political and social sense. For only the United States of America can find the nontotalitarian, nonrevolutionary way to a free industrial society which is the absolutely certain—and at the same time the only—way to overcome totalitarianism.

2.

We know the requirements for a functioning industrial society. In the first place it must give function and status in society to the individual member of the industrial system. It must be capable of integrating the individuals in a social purpose. It must give a social meaning to the purposes, acts, desires and ideals of the individual, and an individual meaning to the organization, institutions and aims of the group.

Secondly, the power in the industrial system must become a legitimate rule. It must derive its authority from a moral principle accepted by society as a legitimate basis of social and political power. And the institutions through which this rulership is exercised must be organized for the realization of the basic purpose of society.

We also know the conditions of freedom. A free society requires political freedom: a controlled, limited, responsible government. It must be organized in its socially constitutive sphere on the basis of the responsible decision of the citizens. It must have self-government. And it is not sufficient to have a purely legal, a purely formal democracy. There must be actual, responsible participation of the citizen in the government and in its decisions.

Finally, in a free society political government and social rule must be separated. Each must be independent of the other. Each must be limited; and one must limit, balance and control the other. Both serve ultimately the same social end. But they must found their authority on different grounds. The basis of political government must be a principle of formal justice; for political institutions are the formal framework of social life. The basis for social rule must be the promise of the fulfillment of a substantial social purpose. For through social rule the substance of society finds its institutional organization. In the juxtaposition of those two principles, in the balance of the institutions based on them, in the control exercised by each of the two legitimate powers over the other, lies the ultimate safeguard of freedom against both anarchy and tyranny.

To establish a free and functioning industrial society, we have to reverse the political and social trends which have dominated the Western world for the last twenty-five, if not for the last fifty, years. During this period the individual has steadily been losing function and status in society. Society has been slowly disintegrating into anarchic masses in all industrial countries. During this period too, the decisive power in the industrial system has lost its legitimate basis. Corporation management has become divorced from individual property rights which had been a good claim to power for two hundred years; and at the same time corporation management emerged as the real master superseding the mercantile rulers of the preindustrial society.

In the political field the trend has been away from the active, responsible participation of the citizen in self-government and toward centralized, uncontrollable bureaucracy. And above all, the absence of a legitimate autonomous rule in society has forced this central bureaucracy of the political sphere to assume the power in the social sphere as well. No other trend of our times seems as "inevitable" as that toward the absolute rule of a paternalistic, bureaucratic state. No other will be as difficult to reverse. At the same time it is the most dangerous of the forces of despotism in our midst. Re-establishment of an autonomous and self-governing social sphere is therefore our most urgent task.

A free and functioning society can be built only if the basically totalitarian tendencies of social disintegration are overcome. But while the trend must be reversed, there can be no restoration of the old preindustrial mercantile society. The nineteenth century is gone forever. It disappeared because it could not socially organize the physical reality of an industrial world. By going back— if it were possible—we could solve not a single one of the problems before us. This realization was the starting point of our analysis; it must also be the starting point of the approach to the future.

The restorer likes to think of himself as a conservative. What he means is that he takes the conditions at a given historical point—for instance those of 1850 or those of 1927—as an absolute. But nothing less conservative could be imagined than this denial of growth and change, of responsibility and decision. To elevate something in the past to the rank of the perfect absolute is just as totalitarian and revolutionary as the Communist or Nazi millennium of the future. In his methods the restorer shows that he is only a totalitarian in disguise. He is as extreme, as ruthless, as contemptuous of historical growth, individual liberty, tradition and existing institutions as the avowed totalitarians. He says "yesterday" where the declared revolutionary says "tomorrow." But there is really no difference between the two absolutist utopias except in political effectiveness. The restorer who preaches that there would be no problems if we could only restore the free-trade system in all its 1860 glory, or the League of Nations Covenant with the amendments proposed in 1924, can only fail. But in his failure he creates the fatal illusion in the minds of the people that there is no alternative other than between reaction and revolution. And in this dilemma the people are only too likely to prefer revolution, with its promise of something new, to the obvious cul-de-sac of reaction.

Restoration of the preindustrial mercantile society not only would not solve the social problems created by the emergence of the industrial system; it would make them insoluble except by slaughter, revolution and tyranny. For any attempt to return to the nineteenth-century society denies the industrial reality of our time. And it is precisely our problem to overcome a revolution by developing industry into the socially constitutive sphere of a functioning and free society.

We have to return to the principles and to the philosophy of the conservative counterrevolution of 1776 and 1787. But we shall have to use these principles for a social integration on a level and with a substance entirely different from the nineteenth century. We have to make industry socially meaningful. We have to build it into the autonomous sphere in which society governs itself in order to fulfill itself. We have, in other words, to organize a physical reality completely different from that of 1776 and 1787. And that means different institutions of society, different organs of social power and control, different social, economic and political problems. The organizing principles are the same, truly conservative principles. But they will have to be used for a new integration of a new society.

We know that the new society must be an industrial society in which industrial life is organized as the socially constitutive sphere. But we do not know what purpose this industrial society will be striving to fulfill, or on what ethical principle it is going to be based. All we know today about the future are the *formal* requirements of a free and functioning society, the conditions without which a society cannot function and without which it cannot be free. But we cannot say to what end the industrial society is to be free, nor what aim its functions are to serve.

The only thing of which we can be reasonably certain

is that the purpose and aim of the industrial society will be different from those of the mercantile society of the nineteenth century. Economic activity will not disappear; nor will it diminish in quantity. In individual life economic success and economic rewards may even remain as important as they are today. And there is no reason to expect a cessation of technical progress. But it is most unlikely that economic activity will be the constitutive social activity, and economic aims the decisive social aims of the industrial society.

It is the very success of the 150 years during which economic goals were uppermost which will tend to relegate these to a secondary place. Economic progress has brought economic abundance within our grasp in the industrial countries. There is therefore no longer any reason to subordinate all social life to economic activity as the mercantile society did. The need is no longer so urgent as to make the gains to be expected from economic advance outweigh every other social consideration. We already have learned to raise the question whether the social price to be paid for an economic achievement is reasonable and justified. In other words, we already have abandoned the belief that economic progress is always and by necessity the highest goal. And once we have given up economic achievement as the highest value and have come to regard it as not more than one goal among many, we have in effect given up economic activity as the basis of social life.

But the abandonment of the economic as the socially constitutive sphere has gone much further. Western society has given up the belief that man is fundamentally Economic Man, that his basic motives are economic motives, and that his fulfillment lies in economic success and economic rewards. The moral concept of the nature and purpose of man on which the mercantile society was based has ceased to be valid. For we have learned that freedom and justice cannot be realized in and through the economic sphere. We have learned that a functioning society can no longer be organized in and through the market. Economic Man has not only made himself superfluous through his material successes; he has also failed politically, socially and metaphysically.*

But while we must assume that Economic Man will not be the concept of man's nature and fulfillment on which the industrial society will be based, and that economic purposes will not be its socially decisive and meaningful purposes, we do not know what substantial ethical purpose and what substantial concept of man's nature will take its place.

---

* I regard this thesis as so completely proven by the war as to require neither further exposition nor documentation. Readers who desire both will find it in my previous book, *The End of Economic Man* (New York and London, 1939).

Hitler has failed in his attempt to impose upon Western society his concept of Heroic Man who finds his fulfillment in permanent war and conquest. Though advertised as an alternative, the Nazi society did not succeed in becoming a functioning society. And of course, it never could become a free society. In the failure of Hitlerism to develop an alternative to mercantile society lies our chance. And to overcome Hitlerism is our task. But we cannot hope to overcome it by restoring the mercantile society. Nor can we hope to be allowed to maintain Economic Man as the concept of man's nature and the basis of our society. We have to develop a free and functioning industrial society on the basis of a new concept of man's nature and of the purpose and fulfillment of society. And we do not and cannot know what this concept will be.

It can be regarded as certain that this concept is already existent in our society. Looking back upon our times fifty years from now, our children will probably marvel at our blindness; in the security of their possession the answer will be as obvious and apparent as it is obscure to us who have to find it. It is probable that the concept of the future society is something all of us know. Probably it is one of the many concepts put forward today as promising a solution. Somebody has the answer; but which of the many proposals made today will prove to have been the one prophetic one, nobody can say. A basic ethical concept of social life cannot be invented; it must be developed. It cannot be manufactured or divined. Above all, there is no knowable way to convert the already latent concept into an effective and acceptable one. All that can be done is to make it possible for such a concept to emerge in a free and nonrevolutionary way. But the emergence of the new concept of man's nature and of society's purpose lies before organized political action or institutional realization. It lies in the philosophical or metaphysical field, in the sphere of beliefs and ideals on which institutions are based but which cannot be realized institutionally or politically.

This absence of a basic social purpose for industrial society constitutes the core of our problem. It makes our times truly revolutionary. It makes cure-alls and short cuts to utopia alluring. But it also makes them doubly dangerous. It explains the attraction of totalitarian doctrines—both rationalist and revolutionary. Yet it makes it all the more important to find a nonrevolutionary unbroken transition from the free and functioning mercantile society to a free and functioning industrial society. And it makes it impossible to effect this transition except in a truly conservative way: from the basis which we have, with tools which we know, and through solving the specific problems in a manner compatible with the known requirements of a free and

functioning society. Any other approach will only lead
to disaster.

3.

As we do not know for what ultimate purpose the
industrial society of the future is to be organized, we
cannot blueprint it. We certainly shall have to develop
a whole set of new social institutions. We shall have
to make drastic changes in our existing institutions.
And we are faced with urgent social and political problems which demand immediate action. Yet we cannot
draw up detailed plans for the future society or build
a small-scale model of it.

The only thing we can do is to subject every proposal
of new social institutions to a rigid test to see whether
it answers our formal minimum requirements for a free
and functioning society. We will have to change and to
reorganize existing institutions so as to make them serv-
iceable as institutions of a free industrial society. And
we can and must shape our course of actions so that
our immediate, day-by-day decisions conform to the conditions which have been developed here as the conditions
for social freedom and social stability.

What we have is a principle of selection between the
various possible courses of action. But it is a purely
negative principle of selection; it enables us to decide
which steps not to take. It does not relieve us of the

basic political decision what to do. We also have a criterion of action; but it is a formal one. We can decide how to use tools—and even, within limits, what tools to use. The sum total of all this is that we have the engineering rules which we must follow in our architecture in order to build the kind of house which we desire. But we cannot pretend that we can visualize the house itself.

Anyone who today presents a complete blueprint admits by implication that he does not understand what the task really is. And an examination of the blueprints will show that in most cases they are nothing more than an attempt at restoration or façade building. A coat of whitewash, however, will not cure the structural defects of the society of our times—as little as a liberal dose of pink or red paint. The "perfect" blueprint is thus doubly deceptive. It not only cannot give the solution; by attempting to conceal the real issues it also makes more difficult their solution.

This does not mean that we shall not have to plan and to prepare our actions in advance. Nothing could be more fatal than to rely on improvisation—which in a situation such as ours is only another word for inertia. We cannot expect to win either the war or the peace by "muddling through"; to trust to luck or inspiration would be a criminal gamble with the dice loaded against us.

We must organize the most comprehensive, the most imaginative and the boldest program of preparations and plans. Yet this planning is the very opposite of the approach advocated today by the large and growing number of "Planners."

"Planning" has become a catchword with a mythical meaning totally different from its ordinary dictionary definition. The panacea which is being advertised today under the misleading name of "Planning" is not a preparation for future events and contingencies. It is the abolition of all limitations on governmental power. The first step of the Planners would be to set up an omnipotent authority with unlimited power to regulate, control, and regiment everything in government and society. The main attack of the Planners is not directed against improvisation and unpreparedness but against the separation of political government from rule in the social sphere. The comprehensive centralized Planning advocated so widely today is first and last a despotism of a "perfect" bureaucracy. The Planners themselves visualize their rule as benevolent and enlightened despotism. They refuse to see that all despotism must degenerate rapidly into rapacious, tyrannical oppression—precisely because it is unlimited, uncontrolled and uncontrollable. But even if a benevolent despotism were possible it would still be incompatible with freedom.

Planning as a philosophy thus rests upon a denial of freedom and upon the demand for the absolute rule of a perfect élite. As a political program it rests upon a provably false assertion: that planning in social, political and economic matters is something new and revolutionary. The Planners assert that nineteenth-century society was anarchic without conscious planning and preparations, and that it trusted entirely to luck and accidents. The claim that we have never before tried to shape our own destiny intelligently is the stock in trade of the Planners.

Actually, the nineteenth century used planning—the proper planning—to an extraordinary extent and with the highest degree of intelligence and conscious purpose. All the basic institutions of the mercantile society grew out of long, careful and deliberate preparation.

The gold standard, for instance, was not the result of accidents but of years of laborious and exhaustive work. It was not anarchy but one of the finest precision machines ever devised. To believe that it just "happened" as the result of natural growth and providential luck is about as sensible as to believe that a herd of monkeys might by accident put together a complete four-engined airplane if let loose in a plane factory. Not only was the purpose which the gold standard was to fulfill worked out deliberately and consciously: to create a monetary and credit system that would be autonomous and independent of the political government. But every single part of this very complicated and highly sensitive mechanism was developed in years of careful search and refinement. Neither the nineteenth-century discount policies nor the system of "Gold Points," nor the ratio between specie and banknotes just "happened" accidentally. The first studies of English banking policy were made in the opening years of the nineteenth century. And the system was completed in the late 1850's with McLeod's researches into credit. Between there was a half century of constant planning, of organized research, and of careful, controlled experimenting.

Equally, America's westward movement was not unplanned and anarchic. Beginning with the Northwestern Ordinance there were a great many careful plans and preparations. Not one of them was final or absolute in character. But all were based on the same basic principles. All were consciously striving to find a solution for the same question: the rapid but orderly organization of new, self-governing communities on new land. The Homestead Act of 1862, which was the climax of this development, was one of the boldest pieces of social engineering ever realized. And the settlement of the Northwest by the transcontinental railways in the 1870's and 1880's was large-scale planning at its most successful.

Similarly, the system of checks and balances or the

English parliamentary system were not accidents but emerged as the result of long, careful and deliberate preparations and experimenting in which many things were tried in order to find institutions able to realize certain definite aims.

Throughout the nineteenth century the extremely valuable and necessary tool of planning and preparing was thus used constantly. But to our modern Planners "Planning" is not a tool that can be used well or badly, that can do some things but not others, that serves the wicked as well as the good. Planning today is proclaimed as the philosopher's stone and as a magical arcanum which automatically solves everything. The tool has been made into an idol; and therewith it loses at once all value as a tool.

The Planning philosophy of today is not a program of preparedness but of unpreparedness. It asks us to give up all possibility of choice, of experimentation and of pragmatic testing in favor of an untried miracle. It demands that we trust in the ability of the twentieth-century "expert" to foretell the future. It starts with a preconceived idea of the future and refuses to provide for anything that does not fit its dogmatic patter. Total Planning is actually total improvisation. It is the renunciation of the deliberate and conscious attempt to work out our problem, in favor of a gamble on the guesses of the technician.

Our planning must therefore be the opposite of that of the Planners. In the first place, we must refute their absolutism. For them there is only one entirely consistent, absolute system; if it be changed in the least particular, chaos becomes inevitable. We, on the other hand, must start with the premise that we do not know where the ultimate solution lies. Hence we must accept inconsistency, variety, compromise and contradictions. We know one thing: the absolutist "either-or" position of the Planners leads to despotism and to nothing else.

Secondly, we cannot rest content with developing plans for the events which we either foresee or want to foresee. We must prepare for all possible—and a good many impossible—contingencies. We must have ready a workable solution—or at least the approach to it—for anything that may come up. And it must be one that fulfills the conditions for the institutions of a free society.

The preparation for the postwar future requires an approach similar to that of a general staff to a future war. The members of the general staff probably have their own ideas on what will happen and also on what should happen. But it would be a poor general staff indeed that confined its work to preparation for probable or desirable contingencies.

The general staff may consider it entirely impossible that there should ever be a war with one of the neighboring countries. Yet it has to prepare for such a war in case its judgment should be faulty. The most efficient general staff is not the one which does the least but that which does the largest amount of unnecessary work. For it is expected to have ready for every conceivable situation a solution which will satisfy the basic principles of strategy—which in their way are just as fixed as are the basic principles of freedom.

Only by preparing for everything that may happen can we hope to prepare ourselves for the one thing that will happen. Even so, only too often we shall find that the actual event lies so far outside anything we had considered possible that we are not prepared for it. But at least by having planned for a great many varied alternatives and even conflicting possibilities we shall have learned enough of the technique and of the practical problems involved to master even the unexpected.

The first requirement for such an approach is that we understand the principles which must govern our preparations and plans. At the same time we must understand as much as possible of the reality which we shall have to master and to organize according to our principles. The central part of this reality is the social system in which we live; and to its understanding this book has been largely devoted. But there are other facts hardly less important. Even before the outbreak of this war the international power-relations and the international economic system had changed so completely as to make impossible any comparison with 1918 or 1929. And, of course, the war is changing the very basis of these spheres. Yet even the apparently boldest of the blueprints is really based on a desire to restore 1913 or to write a better Versailles Peace; however radical on the surface, it is actually outmoded and unimaginative. Before we can even talk about the future, we must know the reality of the present.

For we must start with the present. We can build only with what we have and we cannot begin by inventing what we would like to have. Our first duty is to use our present institutions as much and as well as possible. Only insofar as they cannot be used to constructive purpose—not even after alterations and repairs—are we entitled to replace them with new solutions of our own invention. Even with the most conservative approach, there will still be enough to build and to construct, enough to prune and to cut, to keep an entire generation busy. We shall have to be bold—but never for boldness' sake. We shall have to be radical in our factual analysis and dogmatic in our principles, conservative in our methods and pragmatic in our policies. And above all, we shall have to prevent centralized bureaucratic despotism *by building a genuine local self-government in the industrial sphere.*

4.

The task of building the free and functioning industrial society cannot be postponed until after the war. It is certain that the postwar world will be far more the result of the war society, its institutions, its economic system, its political organization, than of any "postwar policy." If we wait until armistice day with our "postwar plans," we shall be too late. It is not the grandiose schemes of the blueprinters that will determine the structure of postwar society, but the so-called temporary emergency measures of the war—especially if the war should be a long one. They will develop into "temporary emergency measures" of armistice and peace—and they will have become permanent before we even know it.

The facts, institutions and beliefs of this, our present war society will be the foundation of our postwar peace society. They will be the reality with which we have to deal, the institutions which have been developed to deal with it, the social beliefs which motivate our actions. To ignore this, to focus on the moment of armistice or of peace as the one when we shall have to start from new beginnings, is not only a violation of the first principles of political action. It is not only an essentially absolutist approach which fails to see that it will cost as much suffering to remove the "temporary" wartime innovations as it has cost to introduce them. It is also a gross misunderstanding of the limits of political possibility.

It will be simply impossible to start with anything except what we have—especially as time will not stand still and as we shall have a great many immediate and urgent tasks which cannot wait until any new scheme is ready. If we, at this future moment, know what our wartime measures and institutions mean, what they are capable of, what their basic social and political implications are and what we want to use them for, we may have a good chance to do constructive work. If we wait until armistice day to find out, we cannot hope for any success.

It is an even greater mistake to think that the war—this or any other war—is by its nature a threat to our social order or to our free society. It will be a danger only if we let it become one; that is, if we do not use the war to a constructive purpose. Actually, the war might be made into a tremendous opportunity for constructive political action—a much greater one than any we had in the years of the Long Armistice. It offers precisely what our society has been lacking: a social function and status for the individual, and a common social purpose for society. In total war in which everybody is a soldier, everybody has a function; everybody's individual life and work is integrated with the life and work of society—even if the work is only street cleaning or bandage rolling. The activity of every citizen makes sense from the point of view of society; and society is meaningful for every citizen. The will to fight, the drive for victory, the determination to survive as a free nation, give society in the free countries a basic purpose and a social belief the like of which we have not had for a very long time.

That does not mean that war is desirable or that it is enjoyable; it is neither. But it can be made to yield positive results far exceeding the mere defeat of the aggressors. Indeed, it must be made to bear such results unless we are to experience again that frustration, that disillusionment, that moral collapse which after the last war led to the poignant cry that the sacrifices had been wasted. This moral postwar depression would be a real threat to our freedom—not the war itself nor an economic depression after it. And the only way to prevent it is to use the wartime organization of society, the wartime integration of individual and group, the wartime unity of purpose and belief, to develop social institutions of our industrial reality which will hold out a reasonable promise of leading to functioning and free institutions in peacetime.

Such a policy must center on industry. It must be an attempt to develop something we have never had before: social institutions in industry. The fact that in total war the individual in industry has an important social function and a clear and unambiguous social status must be used to build a permanent functioning social organization. The fact that the outcome of the war depends above all on industrial production must be used to develop a legitimate power in industry on the basis of responsible self-government. In other words, the plant must be made into a functioning self-governing social community. It must be made capable of serving industrial society in the same manner in which the village served the rural society and the market the mercantile society.

The guiding principle of such a policy should be to use total war for the establishment of that divorce between political government and autonomous self-government in the social sphere in which freedom so largely rests. We must develop new local and autonomous organs and institutions of self-government to offset the apparently inevitable increase of centralized bureaucratic governmental regimentation in wartime. We must also found nuclei for the growth of an autonomous social sphere and for the limitation of government in the following peacetime.

The answer to the question: how can we escape the political danger of governmental wartime controls, is not a blueprint which pretends to show how to abolish them after the emergency is over. Such plans are certain to remain pure theory. We had better realize from the start that the great bulk of the new controls and of the new centralized bureaucratic administrative agencies is here to stay. We have first to limit the development of such controls as much as is compatible with wartime efficiency; new organs of local self-government must be developed to do as much of the job as possible. Secondly, we must create new organs of responsible self-government—even for old tasks—in order to offset the new centralization and to create a new sphere of freedom.

It has been almost a gospel that total war requires total centralization. But it is a spurious gospel. It is true only for the totalitarian countries. They must be completely regimented, completely centralized, completely controlled because their people cannot be trusted with the slightest particle of responsibility.

The totalitarians cannot afford any self-government; they cannot even afford to allow the least amount of indifference or of tolerance in socially neutral and indifferent spheres. But this compulsion to be totally totalitarian is not a source of strength but one of fatal weakness for the fascist or Nazi systems. To conclude from their experience that the free nations also have to become completely centralized for total war ignores the basic difference between the totalitarians and the free peoples: that they are slaves and we are free. Industrial war such as we are waging today demands not so much an extension of centralized government controls as a shift from old to new methods and organs of political and social management.

We need new political organs to manage consumption and production. But there is no reason why these new political tasks must necessarily be carried out through centralized, bureaucratic government agencies. What is necessary is that centralized action set the frame for new tasks—just as it set the frame, for example through discount and credit policies, for the tasks of the past. The tasks themselves, however, require above all autonomous organs of self-government—both for reasons of wartime efficiency and as a condition of social stability and freedom. Decentralization, self-government and autonomous decisions are fully as much a part of a proper industrial war society as are bureaucratic agencies of the central government. In fact, the effectiveness of a war society under present conditions depends largely upon the extent to which such decentralized responsible self-government can be mobilized.

The central fact in the social crisis of our time is that the industrial plant has become the basic social unit, but that it is not yet a social institution. Power in and over the plant is the basis of social rule and power in an industrial world. Centralized, bureaucratic government has almost succeeded in taking away this power from its former holders, the corporation managers. It is a process comparable in many respects to the breaking of the power of the local barons by the centralized bureaucratic governments of sixteenth- and seventeenth-century Europe. And like the barons the corporation managers are unable to resist.

But freedom could not be maintained if the centralized government should retain the social power; the best that could be hoped for would be an "enlightened" despotism. On the other hand, society could not function if the old managerial rule were restored—provided that such a restoration were at all possible. The only solution which makes possible both a free and a functioning society is the development of the plant into a self-governing community. Industrial society can function only if the plant gives social status and function to its members. And only if the power in the plant is based on the responsibility and decision of the members can industrial society be free. The answer today is neither total planning nor the restoration of nineteenth-century laissez faire, but the organization of industry on the basis of local and decentralized self-government. And the time to start this is now when workers and management, producers and consumers are united in the one purpose of winning the war.

THE END